VALOUR AT VIMY RIDGE

The Great Canadian Victory of World War I

TOM DOUGLAS

Formac Publishing Company Limited
Halifax

Formac Publishing Company Limited recognizes the support of the Province of Nova Scotia through the Department of Communities, Culture and Heritage - Creative Industries Fund. We are pleased to work in partnership with the Province of Nova Scotia to develop and promote our cultural resources for all Nova Scotians. We acknowledge the support of the Canada Council for the Arts, which last year invested $153 million to bring the arts to Canadians throughout the country. This project has been made possible in part by the Government of Canada.

Cover design: Tyler Cleroux

Library and Archives Canada Cataloguing in Publication

Douglas, Tom, 1941-, author
    Valour at Vimy Ridge : the great Canadian victory of
World War I / Tom Douglas.

Previously published: Canmore, Alta.: Altitude Pub., 2007.
Includes bibliographical references and index.
Issued in print and electronic formats.
ISBN 978-1-4595-0485-1 (softcover).--ISBN 978-1-4595-0486-8 (EPUB)

    1. Vimy Ridge, Battle of, France, 1917. 2. World War,
1914-1918--Battlefields--France. 3. World War, 1914-1918--
Canada. I. Title.

D545.V5D68 2017   940.4'31   C2017-903282-8
                                           C2017-903283-6

Formac Publishing Company Limited
5502 Atlantic Street
Halifax, Nova Scotia, Canada
B3H 1G4
www.formac.ca

Printed and bound in Korea.

CONTENTS

To James Ripley Jackson Douglas.
We'll always have Amsterdam!

PROLOGUE

The Prussian officer refused the goodwill gesture with a disdainful wave of his hand. "I understand Canadian cigarettes are made of cattle dung," he said, his clipped English accent hinting at a pre-war British education.

His captors didn't respond, although one of them made an involuntary move with his right hand toward the pistol holstered at his waist. The German smirked at the reaction. "I have also heard Canadians are a collection of drunken cowboys who would shoot an unarmed man without a second thought."

The man's gaze never wavered as he stared at the Canadian officer in charge. "Well, you had better save your ammunition because you will need it. The attack you are planning is the worst-kept secret of the war. It is also the biggest joke the Kaiser has heard in a long time."

The three Canadians in the dimly lit dugout kept silent, not even flinching when another artillery shell shook the foundations, cascading debris down from the rafters. The soldiers appeared content to let their prisoner keep talking. After all, he might blurt out some kernel of information that could save a few lives in the days ahead.

"Your British and French friends tried the same thing and lost over a hundred thousand men," the German continued. "What makes you think a ragtag collection of farmers and fishermen from your country can do any better?"

The Canadian officer in charge made a dismissive sideways gesture with his head, and his two companions grabbed the enemy officer by the arms, preparing to lead him away. He shook off their grasp, pulled his greatcoat tightly around his shoulders, and sneered at his adversary.

"Maybe, just maybe, your men will reach the top of Vimy Ridge," he hissed. "But they will be able to ship the survivors home to Canada in a rowboat."

Introduction
THE WAR TO END ALL WARS

It was also known as the "Great War," but, as with most military slogans, the phrase proved to be both naïve and totally off the mark. History has shown that World War I was not the war that ended all wars — it actually sowed bitter seeds for future conflicts. In addition, with an estimated body count of more than 15 million combatants and civilians, as well as over 22 million wounded, there certainly was nothing great about the bloodbath that lasted from July 28, 1914, until November 11, 1918.

The fuse that set off millions of tonnes of explosives was the assassination of Archduke Franz Ferdinand, heir to the Austro-Hungarian throne, in the Bosnian capital of Sarajevo. When Austro-Hungary blamed Serbia for the assassination and threatened retaliation, Serbia's ally, Russia, began to assemble its troops. Bound by a treaty with Austro-Hungary, Germany considered this mobilization an act of aggression, and declared war on Russia. This brought the allied powers of Great Britain and France into the conflict, lined up with Russia against the central powers led by Germany and Austro-Hungary.

The deadly domino effect caused by a lone assassin would hold the entire world in a death grip of insanity for the next four and a half years — despite the widespread belief from day one that the war would last no more than a few months. Those countries that became engaged in the conflagration would lose an entire generation of their youth, with men and women from all walks of life perishing in the trenches of Flanders and other muddy battlefields across northern Europe.

It would take the combatant countries years to regain what they had lost, both physically and financially — just in time for renewed acts of aggression that would lead to another, and even more devastating, world conflict.

It is difficult to sift historically through the ruins of World War I and come up with anything positive. But one thing Canada gained from participating in this barbarous affair was a sense of pride at having stood shoulder to shoulder with some of the most powerful nations on earth to defeat a common enemy. And that sense of pride began to take shape on April 9, 1917, at the Battle of Vimy Ridge.

Chapter 1
INNOCENCE LOST

Church bells rang. People danced in the streets. Brass bands played martial music as zealous youths shouldered wooden rifles and marched through town to the cheers and applause of adoring crowds. Recruiters turned a blind eye as young boys barely into their teens lied about their age so they could sign up to go overseas and fight against the Hun.

This was the nationalistic fever that gripped Canada in the summer of 1914 when war was declared against Germany. Since Confederation in 1867, Canadians had experienced little in the way of armed conflict other than sending a battalion of avolunteers to assist Great Britain in the Boer War in 1899. That three-year conflict in South Africa involved some 7,000 Canadians, including 12 women nurses, and resulted in 267 Canadian fatalities. It had been considered a noble cause, and the romance of battle had

Second contingent from Saskatoon, SK, leaving for training, then overseas, 1915.

grown in the minds of most Canadians every year since. By 1914, when war clouds were forming over Europe, the majority of able-bodied males from Victoria to Halifax were ready, in fact eager, to fight for king and country.

The Canadian government — perhaps realizing that the country was ill prepared militarily, with a militia numbering just over 3,000 and a fledgling navy — had been little more than lukewarm in its official reaction to the situation overseas. When Britain declared war against Germany on August 4, 1914, Canada issued this statement: "If unhappily war should ensue, the Canadian people will be united ... to maintain the honour of the empire."

But a groundswell of patriotism flared up across the land like a grass fire on a tinder-dry prairie and, by August 10, authorization had been granted for the formation of the Princess Patricia's Canadian Light Infantry Regiment. The regiment was named after the only daughter of the then-serving governor general of Canada, Prince Arthur, the Duke of Connaught, who was the third son of Queen Victoria. The ranks of the PPCLI were filled in just over a week, made up for the most part of trained ex-regular soldiers who had served in the British army during the Boer War. The PPCLI was financed privately, mainly by Captain Hamilton Gault of Montreal. On December 21, 1914, the regiment, under the command of the governor general's military secretary Colonel F.D. Farquhar DSO, set foot on French soil and was the first Canadian unit committed to battle.

Back home, volunteers continued to pour into the recruiting stations and, by late September, more than 30,000 hastily trained soldiers marched out of the Valcartier mobilization camp near Quebec City to board trains for the East Coast. On October 1, officers and men stomped proudly up the gangplank of 33 ocean liners — including the RMS *Olympic*, sister ship to the RMS *Titanic* — and set sail for England under the protection of British Royal Navy escort ships. It was the largest convoy ever to cross the Atlantic. The enthusiastic Canadians crowded the railings of these transport ships as the flotilla came within sight of the English coast.

The Rugged Reality
It would not take long for that enthusiasm to wane. Once the gigantic task of offloading men and equipment had been accomplished, the troops found themselves in far less than pleasant surroundings on Salisbury Plain. They comprised the 1st Canadian Infantry Division, under the command of a British officer, Lieutenant General E.A.H. Alderson, and they soon woke up to the reality of army life. Salisbury Plain is a cold, windswept, and perpetually rain-drenched chalk

plateau of about 780 square kilometres in south-central England. Conditions there were far more rugged than anything the soldiers had experienced in Canada. The training was exhausting, as every effort was expended to get these "green" Canadians into shape for the fighting ahead.

The 1st Division crossed the English Channel in February 1915 and immediately saw action at Ypres, Belgium. Over a two-week period, the Canadians learned the realities of warfare, suffering 5,500 casualties. But the determined troops kept on coming. The 2nd Canadian Infantry Division was formed in Great Britain in May 1915 with the influx of a huge contingent of troops from Canada. This new division was pressed into service in September and spent a long and bitterly cold winter in Belgium. Their ranks would be severely bloodied in six major battles in 1916.

With two divisions of Canadians overseas, the Canadian Corps was formed on September 13, 1915, with General Alderson in command. The 3rd Division was added to the Corps in December 1915 and the 4th Division in April 1916. A 5th Division would be organized later, but it was used strictly for guard duty in Great Britain.

Tragedy and a clash of personalities resulted in several high-level changes in command within the Corps before the Canadians arrived in the Vimy area late in 1916. The 3rd Division's commanding officer, Brigadier General Malcolm Smith Mercer, was the victim of "friendly fire" at Mount Sorrel near the Belgian town of Ypres when shrapnel from a wayward British artillery shell pierced his heart. He went into the history books with the dubious distinction of being the highest-ranking Canadian officer killed in action in World War I.

Women Operators, *a painting by Canadian artist George Andrew Reid, 1919. Of the almost 300,000 factory workers engaged in Allied war production in 1917, approximately one in eight was a woman.*

The 1st Division CO, Brigadier General Arthur Currie, took on the added responsibilities of commander of the entire Canadian Corps upon the sacking of General Alderson by Canadian Minister of Militia and Defence Sir Sam Hughes. When the Corps suffered 1,300 casualties at the battles of St. Eloi in April 1916, Hughes, who was openly hostile toward Alderson, is thought to have seized upon this disaster as an excuse to dump the Corps commander. Hughes himself would soon be replaced, largely because of his abrasive, bull-headed way of conducting the affairs of war.

With such major battles as St. Eloi, Ypres, Mount Sorrel, and Sanctuary Wood, the raw recruits who had flocked to the recruiting stations back in Canada were battle-hardened and embittered soldiers before two years had passed. Government censors, by slashing newspaper accounts of the carnage at the front and by blacking out most of the text of letters from the troops to their family and friends, would keep the naïve townsfolk back home pretty

Canadians in training on Salisbury Plain, England, 1915. Mud like the mud to come.

much in the dark about the horrors their young people were suffering. And because they still had no idea what they were in for, able-bodied Canadians continued to believe the propaganda and flock to the recruiting stations.

Those patriotic young men who had dreamed of glory in a far-off land during the heady summer days of 1914, and those who followed in the ensuing months, soon found that they had been sold a bill of goods. There was nothing glorious about seeing the man next to you blown to bits by an enemy mortar shell. And the stirring strains of the military march you'd heard as you paraded down the main street of your home town were blotted out of your memory by the incessant roar of artillery, the screech of an incoming mortar shell, and the chatter of death-dealing machine guns.

But as terrifying as actual combat might be, it was often a welcome respite from existing like an animal in the filthy, disease-laden trenches that scarred the once bucolic landscape of northern France and Belgium. Skirmishes were fought that might gain one side or the other a few metres of territory, but this victory was usually short-lived, with the enemy coun-terattacking a few hours later and taking back what ground they had lost. Life in the muddy, shell-pummelled fields of northeastern Europe was a horrible nightmare, worse than anything imaginable. It was a nightmare from which there was no awakening and one that it seemed would end in death — or a disfiguring wound that was a ticket home.

Major-Gen. Malcolm Mercer was the highest-ranking CEF officer to be killed in action. It was "friendly fire."

World War I, unlike any conflict before or since, turned into a huge stalemate with the opposing sides sometimes less than 25 metres apart, living like mud-encrusted moles in a vast series of ditches and tunnels.

Trench warfare, according to those who lived through it, was hell on earth.

Chapter 2
TRENCH WARFARE

The recruiting posters and rah-rah newsreels painted a romantic view of what it was like to go to war. The poster boys were clean-cut lads dressed in freshly pressed uniforms sipping wine at outdoor cafés in Paris. The French mesdemoiselles sitting with them were breathtakingly beautiful, and they gazed adoringly at these conquering heroes who had driven the beastly enemy from their country.

There were no scenes of a corpse-strewn no man's land — that stretch of barren ground that separated the trenches of the antagonists. No close-ups of a diseased rat crawling over your face as you tried desperately to grab a few hours' sleep before having to go "over the top" to raid the enemy trench just metres away from yours. No mention of a German sniper waiting for you to emerge from the relative safety of a muddy shell hole so that he could blow your head off. No depiction of life in the trenches, where foot rot, lice, and the stench of death were your constant companions.

Trench warfare, a unique World War I phenomenon in which opposing troops would play deadly cat and mouse games with a nearby enemy for weeks and months on end, became the norm after the bloody Battle of the Marne in September 1914. That epic confrontation dashed the plans of the German army to capture nearby

Canadians at home were urged to Carry On! Buy Victory Bonds!

Paris. Forced to retreat north to the River Aisne, General Erich von Falkenhayn ordered his troops to dig trenches to protect themselves from advancing British and French forces.

When the Allies realized that the German trenches were formidable obstacles that could not be readily overtaken, they too began digging in. After a few months, these opposing trenches stretched from the North Sea to the Swiss frontier. For the next three years, neither side was able to advance more than a few kilometres along this line that came to be known as the Western Front. But living conditions in what amounted to little more than deep ditches wasn't anything like the cozy bungalows or college dorms or rural family homesteads the young Canadians had left behind. Even a trapper's shack in Canada's wild North seemed like a

A Canadian poster aimed at recruiting Canadian Jews. There was also an English-language version of this same poster.

palace to those dug in on the cruel fields of northern France and Belgium.

War diarists, historians, and dramatists, in hindsight, have minutely detailed the daily life of the common soldier — British, French, Canadian, and German — on the Western Front. It is not a pretty picture. But no story about World War I — and

18

Sleep when you can. Canadians in the front line trenches, February 1918.

in particular the magnificent achievement of the Canadians at Vimy Ridge — would be complete without a basic understanding of these inhuman and seemingly insurmountable obstacles that had to be overcome on the road to victory.

Life In The Trenches

The excavations along the Western Front were built in threes — the front-line, support, and reserve trenches. This trio of long, snake-like ditches covered between 220 and 550 metres of ground from front to back and could wind for several kilometres across the terrain parallel to the enemy fortifications. They were not dug in a straight line because the occupants needed the relative safety of a sharp turn to hide behind so they could draw a bead on an approaching enemy soldier if their trench was overtaken.

Running perpendicular to these channels were communication trenches for fresh troops, equipment, and supplies to move up to the line and wounded soldiers to be taken to the rear. The trenches were about 2.5 metres deep by 2 metres wide. The front lip of the excavation was known as the parapet, while the rear area was called a parados. Each was protected by a stack of sandbags to absorb bullets and shell fragments.

The trench was too deep to allow its occupants to see over the top, so a small ledge called a fire-step was added. The soldiers would crouch down on this protrusion, then pop up to take potshots at the enemy before ducking down quickly to avoid having their heads blown off by a camouflaged sniper who'd been lying motionless for hours in no man's land. Officers would also make use of hand-held periscopes to monitor enemy troop movements.

Poking their heads over the parapet to see what the other side was doing took the lives of many a young arrival at the front. The more seasoned soldiers tried to warn newcomers to keep their heads down while in the trenches, but curiosity would often take hold and these wet-behind-the-ears troops would take a tentative peek over the top of the trench. Their first sight of the enemy would usually be their last. Snipers were lying in wait on both sides for the foolhardy to expose themselves. One favourite trick of the Germans was to fly a kite with English writing on it above their front lines. If an Allied

A German soldier beyond human aid. Vimy Ridge, April 1917.

soldier forgot himself and craned his neck to read the lettering, he never got a chance to do it a second time.

The front-line trenches were protected by gigantic bales of barbed wire placed far enough forward to prevent the enemy from getting within grenade-lobbing distance. So impenetrable and tangled were these obstacles that they acted like the steel web of a monstrous spider, impaling any hapless soldier who came close enough to get tangled in the trap. Before a battle, troops would be sent out with wire cutters to chop a path through this razor-sharp wire. It was one of the more hazardous duties to perform because of those ever-present snipers. Pre-battle attempts by the artillery to obliterate the wire were met with disdain by experienced soldiers, who had learned the hard way that this only blew the entanglement up in the air. When it

Canadian Grenadier Guards in a trench at Armentiers, February 1915.

landed intact back on the ground, it was even more tightly wound together, and thus more impenetrable.

Short ditches just over 30 metres long were dug toward the enemy position from the front-line trenches. Called "saps" — with those who dug them referred to as sappers — they were used by small advance parties of soldiers as listening posts. After an enemy bombardment, the newly formed shell craters also served this purpose. But the snipers knew this as well, and they waited silently for hapless soldiers to try to reach one of these holes only to be added to the notches on the snipers' rifle butts.

Strategic Advantage

The Germans, being the first troops to dig in after the Battle of the Marne, had the advantage of selecting the most strategically advantageous positions on the high

Wash when you can. Swimming in a shell hole behind Canadian lines, June 1917.

ground. Not only did this allow them a better field of vision, it also forced the attacking Allies to charge uphill while loaded down with weapons and equipment that made their assaults that much more difficult to carry out. Moreover, with the French, British, and Canadian trenches only a few feet above sea level, the Allied troops would find themselves standing ankle deep in water after digging down only a few centimetres. Waterlogged trenches meant wet feet for days and weeks on end — and wet feet led to frostbite or the dreaded trench foot that, if left untreated, could result in amputation.

When tens of thousands of troops were incapacitated with trench foot early in the conflict, the Allies issued an order that each soldier was to massage his feet vigorously first thing in the morning, then wash them thoroughly. Fresh water was scarce and this often meant using the brackish water in a shell hole behind the lines. Next came an application of grease

Write home when you can. This 29th Canadian Infantry Battalion, 2nd Division soldier wears a "Gor Blimey" trench cap. July 1916.

made from whale oil to keep the dampness out. In addition, the troops were ordered to carry three pairs of dry socks with them at all times and to change their socks at least twice a day. Failure to comply, as would be evidenced by an outbreak of trench foot, was punishable by court martial.

Dysentery was another killer that accounted for thousands of deaths in the trenches. Needless to say, sanitary conditions in these waterlogged ditches were appalling. Latrines were dug behind the lines, but these soon filled up and spilled into the trenches. In addition, many of those excavations had been dug in areas where corpses from earlier battles had been hastily buried, and the decaying bodies were another source of deadly germs. For that matter, the battlefields were located mainly on destroyed farmland, where the soil had been fertilized with manure for centuries. Deadly microbes infested the ground and contaminated wounds, causing gangrene, a horrible affliction that often proved fatal in the days before wonder drugs.

A steady diet of canned beef, mouldy biscuits, boiled sweets, and coffee made from ground turnips left the men susceptible to boils, scabies, and other skin eruptions. And there was no popping down to the local drugstore to select a tube of some soothing ointment that would cure whatever the ailment might be.

As can be expected, a great number of soldiers on both sides of the line suffered mental breakdowns from the days, weeks, and months of living under abominable conditions, with the risk of death or disfigurement a constant concern. The term "shell shock" was coined to describe this affliction, but many officers — and even a number of battlefield doctors — refused to accept this as a reason for taking the victims off

What a barbed-wire entanglement looked like. Three hard-to-find crucifixes mark graves of three Canadians, buried where they died trying to cross the German barbed wire.

German trenches might be better-built than the Canadians', but lice infested them, too. Soldiers from both sides had to pick lice.

the front lines. As a result, many a disturbed soldier would deliberately mutilate himself in order to get a "blighty" — a wound that would send him to England for recuperation and, if he were really lucky, home for good.

There were others whose minds completely snapped and they would commit suicide rather than live one more day in the hellhole of a front-line trench. Refusing to obey a direct order, they would be shot by one of the senior officers. Or they would deliberately raise their heads above the rim of the trench and let a sniper do the job. The truly desperate would take off one boot and sock, point their rifle at their heads, and pull the trigger with their big toe.

The rallying cry "for king and country" soon took on a cynical overtone.

Chapter 3
EASTER MOURNING

Among those keeping the home fires burning in Canada, all but the most dedicated optimists had little to rejoice about on Easter weekend in early April 1917. The Canadian Corps had been overseas for more than a year and the news from the front had been anything but encouraging. Not only had the Allies suffered major setbacks in a number of bloody battles, but the arrival of that dreaded bearer of bad tidings — the "We-Regret-To-Inform-You" telegram — was becoming a far-too-common occurrence across the land.

One ray of hope was that the United States had finally declared war on Germany on Good Friday, but it would be weeks, and probably months, before the Yanks could get mobilized and begin landing their soldiers "over there." Furthermore, there were rumours in the press and from wounded soldiers repatriated to Canada that a major offensive

Sheet music for patriotic songs were featured in the 1917 Eaton's catalogue.

was imminent. Many a churchgoer that Easter Sunday prayed that their loved ones would not be involved in a bloodbath, or, if they ended up being part of a major assault, that they be spared serious injury or death and would soon be coming home.

Meanwhile, people from coast to coast tried to get along in their daily lives as best they could — putting thoughts of muddy battlefields and disease and death out of their minds by concentrating on happier things. Music lovers waited eagerly for the promised May 31 release of the first jazz recording, "The Darktown Strutters Ball." They read the newspaper advertisements and wondered whether they could afford that new table-model being offered for $25 by Toronto's Regal Phonograph Company.

Others bought up the sheet music to such catchy new tunes as "For Me and My Gal," "I'm Always Chasing Rainbows," and "Oh Johnny Oh Johnny Oh." While they were waiting to pay for their purchases, they gossiped about the death on April 1 of ragtime composer Scott Joplin, who had written such lively pieces as "The Maple Leaf Rag" and "The Entertainer."

Movie fans waited patiently for the arrival at the local cinema of silent-screen star Theda Bara's new hit, *Cleopatra*, and Canada's own Mary Pickford's *Rebecca of Sunnybrook Farm*. And, if you really wanted to forget your troubles, there was a new release called "His Wedding Night," starring those two hilarious comics Buster Keaton and Fatty Arbuckle.

For the literary crowd, McClelland, Goodchild and Stewart had just published the fifth novel in Lucy Maud Montgomery's popular series about the beloved Anne Shirley called *Anne's House of Dreams*. And the April edition of the *National Geographic* — available at 25 cents a copy, or $2.50 a year — offered such articles as "The Burden France Has Borne" and "Friends of our Forests."

Cleopatra (Theda Bara) and Caesar (Fritz Leiber) in the hit movie.

While parts of the country were still gripped in the icy fingers of a brutal Canadian winter, newspaper photographs showed publicity hounds attempting to fry an egg on the sidewalks of New York. The weatherman had played an April Fool's Day joke by handing the city the hottest April 1 on record at 28 degrees Celsius.

31

A magazine ad for Mary Pickford in Rebecca of Sunnybrook Farm.

If the more prescient members of Canadian society slept fitfully after bedding down when the traditions of Easter Sunday 1917 had been observed, there was good reason for it. Because of the time difference between Canada and Europe, when they awoke Easter Monday morning it was

Land Girls Hoeing. *Painted by Manly MacDonald in 1919 for the Canadian War Memorials Fund, it shows young women who volunteered for Ontario's Farm Service Corps. They wear loose-fitting garments to accommodate the heavy labour involved in working the land and broad-brimmed hats to protect against the sun. In 1918, 2,400 such women assisted fruit farmers in the Niagara region.*

already afternoon overseas. Since they'd pulled the covers over themselves and turned off the lights, several thousand of their countrymen had been killed and more than double that number wounded in northern France on a small knoll with the innocuous-sounding name of Vimy Ridge.

A Canadian wartime fundraising poster depicts three French women pulling a plow. This is the English-language version.

Chapter 4
A RIDGE TOO FAR

The troops of the Canadian Corps were well aware that a major offensive would be launched that spring against the German stronghold of Vimy Ridge. They just didn't know exactly when. Then a message was circulated through the ranks that let them know it would be a matter of hours or days, at most.

> Under the orders of your devoted officers, in the coming battle you will advance or fall where you stand facing the enemy. To those who will fall, I say: You will not die, but step into immortality. Your mothers will not lament your fate, but will be proud to have borne such sons. Your name will be revered forever and ever by your grateful country, and God will take you unto Himself.

Major General Arthur Currie
Commander, 1st Division
Canadian Corps
Special Order before Vimy Ridge
March 27, 1917

Currie could be excused if his hand trembled a bit as he signed that order. They were brave words he wrote, but if he believed them, he was one of the few officers in the Allied High Command who did. The British and French had earlier tried to wrest the strategic hump of land near the city of Arras in northern France from a seasoned German force that had held it since October 1914. When the smoke of battle

Sir Arthur Currie in July, 1917. He was promoted to Lt.-Gen. and knighted in the field by King George V after Vimy Ridge was won.

German shells bursting near dug-in Canadian troops. Though an officer stands, most of the men keep lower. Vimy Ridge is that insignficant hump on the horizon, to the right. April 1917.

cleared, there were well in excess of 150,000 British and French casualties, including 20,000 dead. The flatland in front of the 61-metre-high ridge and the slopes leading to the top were strewn with the rotting corpses of Allied soldiers.

It had been an open secret for some time that the Canadians would be thrown into the fray next. Vimy Ridge was an essential stretch of land — the cork in the bottle to Allied advances aimed at pushing the enemy out of France and into total defeat. British and French officers warned the Canadians that taking the ridge was an impossible task. The Germans were not only solidly dug in to a zigzag of deep trenches that furrowed the limestone and chalk ridge for several kilometres, but they had also constructed a series of tunnels and underground caves they could retreat to when

German trenches were on higher ground, and drier, and tended to be better-built than the Canadians'. The Germans intended to stay.

artillery shelling became particularly heavy. German officers openly sneered at the prospect of an amateur army, thrown together by Canada after war had been declared, being able to succeed where the seasoned professional soldiers of Great Britain and France had failed. French General Robert Nivelle considered the Canadian attack an exercise that would come to nothing.

Meticulous Planning

If Currie had any doubt about the ability of the Canadian Corps to capture Vimy Ridge as part of the upcoming Battle of Arras, he kept it to himself. He and his staff had been planning months in advance for a lightning attack aimed at overrunning the German positions in one day, with a brief mop-up action the following morning. It has been said that no Allied offensive

Trenches behind the Canadians at Vimy Ridge. Both sides had observers in kite balloons to photograph the opponents.

on the Western Front was more exhaustively planned than the assault on Vimy Ridge.

Currie and other senior officers realized that earlier defeats, especially where frontal assaults had been made on what seemed to be an invincible enemy position, had resulted from old-fashioned military thinking. A lack of preparation and a refusal to let the troops know in advance exactly what they were expected to do had been blueprints for disaster. "Take time to train them," Currie advised and his superiors, fortunately, listened to him. For instance, Sir Julian Byng, the British lieutenant general selected to command the Canadian contingent overseas, told his officers: "What I want is the discipline of a well-trained pack of hounds … Never lose sight of your objective. Reach it in your own way."

Lt.-Gen. Sir Julian Byng.

It was obvious that both Byng and Currie cared greatly for their men and were much admired in return. Members of the Canadian Corps referred to themselves as Byng's Boys, after a popular British music hall ditty of the time. The story buzzed along the trenches about this casual officer being reprimanded by King George V for wearing shabby uniforms. He also didn't stand on ceremony in a number of areas, including the protocol of saluting. Strolling along with his hands in his pockets, he would often return a salute by raising his pocketed hand as high as it would go within the confines of his greatcoat.

For his part, Currie, unlike many of his fellow generals within the Allied forces, refused to consider front-line troops as mere cannon fodder. He did everything he could to keep casualties down. In his book *Adventure*, Major General J.E.B. Seely, commanding officer of the Canadian Cavalry Brigade, praised Currie's people skills.

"Of all the men that I knew in nearly four years on the Western Front, I think Currie was the man who took the most care of his men," Seely wrote. "Moreover, again and again he nearly brought his career to an end by bluntly refusing to do things which he was certain would result in loss of life without compensating advantage."

Canadians were trained before the battle in using captured weapons. Here, Canadian artillerymen fire a German 4.2 inch howitzer.

In order to plan the attack properly, a full-scale mock-up of Vimy Ridge was built behind Allied lines. This simulated battlefield was festooned with coloured tape and flags signifying where each unit of the Corps was to be deployed and what its objective was. Every soldier who would take part in the actual assault was drilled and redrilled for weeks on the role he would play in the upcoming attack, from the time he went over the top until his unit's objective was taken. Unlike so many battles where the troops were kept in the dark about what was to take place, each man, from private to senior officer, was given a map of the area he would be traversing. Furthermore, every soldier was trained to perform a number of tasks and, if necessary, take command of his unit. In that way, when others in the group were killed or wounded, there were instant replacements to maintain the momentum. The troops were also taught to operate German weapons so they could turn them on the enemy once the weapons were captured.

Surprising the Enemy

Working stealthily, tunnelling crews built underground networks beneath no man's land with explosive charges that could be detonated during the battle so that waves of Canadian troops could pour out of the tunnels and overwhelm a surprised enemy in nearby trenches. A series of subways was constructed seven metres underground that would allow assault troops to move to their jumping-off points while protected from shelling. The subways would also allow the wounded to be evacuated from the battlefield. Chambers for brigade and battalion headquarters were cut into the walls of the subways. Some of these excavations were also designed as ammunition stores, communications centres, and dressing stations.

In preparation for the attack, Canadian and British engineers made improvements to the existing roadwork in the Corps' forward area and added several kilometres of new plank road. In addition, they repaired bombed-out tramways so that light trains, powered by mules, horses, or gasoline engines could transport the many tonnes of rations, stores, and ammunition required at the front on a daily basis. Artillery shells assigned to the Vimy operation totalled 38,250 tonnes. Additional pipeline was laid to carry the Corps' daily requirement of 2.3 million litres of water to the soldiers and some 50,000 animals, as well as for cooling overheated artillery pieces. Canadian signallers installed 34 kilometres of cable two metres underground to withstand enemy shelling.

Almost ready for the first use, a light railroad is built for Vimy Ridge. The railroad will carry supplies up, and wounded back.

The Allied High Command knew from the earlier bitter defeats of the French and British and from intelligence reports made during the early months of 1917 that the Canadians didn't have much hope of success. For one thing, the ridge was a strong link in the chain of German defences, so the enemy would fight bitterly to retain it.

The ridge provided the Germans with an excellent vantage point from which to lob a constant barrage of artillery shells at the nearby French-held city of Arras. Furthermore, it was a stronghold connecting the main Hindenburg Line (stretching nearly 160 kilometres from Lens, near Arras, to the Aisne River, near Soissons) to the German defence systems running north to the coast of the English Channel.

The Germans had been augmenting the fortifications on the ridge since capturing it in October 1914. Both slopes of the outcropping gave the defenders a decided advantage. The eastern side away from the Canadian trenches was a tangle of forests where a number of large artillery pieces could be hidden. Since the incline on the west facing the Canadians was gradual, a large number of the assault troops would have to attack over open ground — and become prime targets for artillery, machine-gun, and rifle fire. The Canadians faced three main defensive lines comprised of heavily fortified trenches, concrete machine-gun posts, and walls of skin-slicing barbed wire. The Germans would also be well insulated against artillery barrages in deep dugouts and vast underground chambers, some of which could shelter entire battalions.

Sticking Together

One of the vital keys to success at Vimy, Currie kept insisting, was that the Canadians would be fighting side by side with men they had known since enlisting, or earlier. Where in the past Canadian troops had been scattered among a number of British units, Currie, with Byng's support, insisted on bringing the various Canadian battalions together for this important battle under the four divisions that comprised the Canadian Corps. There were about 40,000 troops from the Corps training for the attack, with some 20,000 picked to go "over the top" in the first wave.

Australian General Sir John Monash would praise this tactic in writing about Vimy years later. "It is impossible to overrate the advantages which accrued to the Canadian Corps from the close and constant association of all four divisions with the others," he maintained.

Front Line — at Night, by J.A. Churchman, c. 1918. Because movement by daylight was so dangerous, nights were frantic: light was an enemy.

While it was true that the Canadians had pretty well started from scratch in building their armed forces at the outbreak of war in the summer of 1914, their ground troops received a brutal baptism under fire in several subsequent encounters on French soil. Particularly costly in terms of casualties was the bloody Battle of the Somme in 1916, where more than 24,000 Canadian troops were killed or wounded.

It was at the Somme that the Canadians earned a reputation as a force to be reckoned with. As British Prime Minister Lloyd George wrote, "The Canadians played a part of such distinction that thenceforward they were marked out as storm troopers; for the remainder of the war they were brought along to head the assault in one great battle after another. Whenever the Germans found the Canadian Corps coming into the line they prepared for the worst."

Ever since the Canadian arrival in the Vimy area shortly after the Somme offensive, the Corps' casualty rate had been high. One preliminary attack against a section of the ridge on March 1, 1917, cost the Canadians 687 lives. Two of these fatalities were the commanding officers of their units — Lieutenant Colonel Samuel Gustavfus Beckett of Toronto, who was in charge of the 75th Battalion, and Lieutenant Colonel Arnold Kemball of the 54th, who hailed from the village of Kaslo, British Columbia.

In total, some 1,400 Canadian officers and men were killed or injured in the time leading up to the major assault on the ridge. Withering machine-gun and sniper fire cut down most of them as they raided German trenches seeking prisoners who could provide valuable information for the upcoming attack.

This information-gathering tactic involved sending small patrols into no man's land under cover of darkness. These raiders had to slither forward on their stomachs through mud, decaying corpses, severed limbs, abandoned weapons, and field rations, as well as foraging rats feeding on the carnage of earlier battles. Their biggest prize was an enemy sentry they could bring back for interrogation. Their biggest fear was a German rocket that, when fired into the sky, would release a flare on a small parachute that turned the blackest of nights into broad daylight and exposed them to snipers and machine-gunners.

There were other ways that the Allied planners gathered intelligence on German troop strength, weaponry, and the strongholds that would have to be immobilized before the Vimy assault. Tunnels were dug under the enemy

A kite balloon climbs after launch. An observer would be in the basket below, and able to send down messages about what he saw.

lines and listening devices were installed to pick up bits of information from troops talking to each other or officers planning their next move.

Spy in the Sky

Both sides used observation balloons filled with gas or hot air to spy on their adversaries. Several of these devices, each containing an observer to spy on the enemy, were winched into the air at the same time so that comparative sightings could be made and wire mesh could be dangled between the balloons to hamper the manoeuvrability of enemy aircraft bent on blowing them out of the sky. It was not so easy to bring down a balloon. Standard bullets would usually pass right through the fabric. Special incendiary or explosive bullets were needed and an attacking pilot would have to be careful not to get too enthusiastic and follow a descending balloon that was being rapidly winched to the ground. Such carelessness could bring his aeroplane into range of enemy anti-aircraft fire.

Setting an observation balloon aflame — which generally meant a fiery death or a fatal leap from the gondola by the device's occupant — was regarded as a legitimate "kill" by the various air forces involved in the war. One of Canada's World War I aces, Billy Bishop, got his start on winning a chestful of awards by earning a Military Cross over Vimy on April 7, 1917, for destroying a balloon. Bishop and his fellow Royal Flying Corps pilots also contributed to the Vimy victory by shooting down enemy aircraft that, like the German balloons, had been sent aloft to learn what they could about the Canadians' intentions. In addition, the RFC fliers were able to assist the Canadian Corps' couter-battery unit in destroying more than 80 percent of the Germans' heavy guns prior to the attack by flying over the German lines and taking aerial photographs of the gun emplacements. They would also provide air support during the battle and, through a flag system employed by the ground troops, report the successful capture of enemy strongholds by the various attack units.

Of course, while the Canadians were attempting to gain as much information about enemy troop strength as possible before the final assault, the Germans were also curious about what the Corps was up to. With the advantage of being on higher ground than the Canadians, they had a panoramic view of what was going on below. To make the enemy's task more difficult, Corps engineers

Firing a heavy. A Canadian BL 12-inch Mk. I railway howitzer in action during the Battle of Vimy Ridge.

erected wooden poles on either side of the roads in the front-line area and strung great swaths of coarse jute fabric between them. From the German positions on the ridge, the hessian material resembled the road surface and gave the false impression that nothing was going on, while supply vehicles streamed back and forth underneath. That ruse worked so well that scrim netting, interwoven with bits of coloured cloth, was draped over the rail lines, giving free movement to rail cars beneath.

A Severe Pounding

All hell was let loose on March 20, 1917, in preparation for the upcoming attack. In order to pulverize the entrenched Germans, artillery units from Canada, Britain, and South Africa unleashed a continuous barrage from more

Empty shell casings, collected after a major bombardment of the German lines.

than 375 heavy guns and howitzers, as well as more than 700 pieces of field artillery. It was the largest such barrage in history up to that point. At the same time, the detonation of tonnes of explosives that had been deposited in freshly dug tunnels under the German positions added to the mayhem. All of this was aimed at not only destroying as many enemy gun emplacements as possible, but also crippling the morale of the German soldiers who were forced to cower in their trenches and tunnels while the Allied shells rained down on them.

The non-stop shelling continued for more than 10 days and then, as abruptly as it had begun, it ceased. This tactic was another attempt to shatter the spirits of the enemy. Just when they might have thought the worst was over, an even greater artillery offensive was launched on April 2. From then until April 9, a period of time the Germans would later refer to as "the week of suffering," about a million shells — 50,000 tonnes of explosives — pounded the German defences.

The brilliance of a young electrical engineering graduate from McGill University was largely responsible for the success of the Canadian artillery campaign in the lead-up to the Battle of Vimy Ridge. Lieutenant Colonel Andrew McNaughton was given carte blanche by Sir Julian Byng to come up with innovations that would bring artillery into the 20th century. McNaughton was named counter-battery staff officer and fine tuned calculation of the position of the enemy's big guns by observing the muzzle flashes and timing the sound of a shell from the instant it was fired until it hit its target.

This method of pinpointing an enemy artillery piece was based on the findings of a French gunner, Charles Nordmann, who had been an astronomer for the Paris Observatory. In the autumn of 1914, Nordmann worked out a formula for locating the precise position of an enemy field piece by measuring the difference in time required for the sound of the guns firing to reach strategically placed microphones. He discussed his theory with French physicist Lucien Bull, who designed the required equipment.

The idea worked well in the laboratory, but it took more than a year and a half for the necessary equipment to be developed for field conditions. British artillery began using the microphones and measuring devices in the summer of 1916 and passed the information along to McNaughton.

Each Allied sound-ranging unit consisted of a minimum of six microphones spread out at precise intervals behind the front-line trenches connected to headquarters. An operator located in a listening post well forward of the microphones would press a key when he heard an enemy gun firing. This action would start a recording back at headquarters of the report from the artillery piece. The sound experts could then determine the gun's location from the time intervals between the microphones. It was then up to the Allied artillery to zero in on the enemy artillery piece and put it out of commission.

McNaughton also developed a system for keeping track of the wear and tear on the barrels of the heavy guns so that they could be replaced before they started losing their accuracy. Another innovation that McNaughton was quick to embrace was the use of a new fuse that would explode shells on impact rather than in the air above a target. This new technique blew holes three or four metres wide in the thickly coiled rolls of German barbed wire that had previously trapped attacking soldiers, turning them into sitting ducks for enemy snipers.

Perhaps McNaughton's greatest contribution to the Battle of Vimy Ridge was his implementation of the creeping barrage. This was a technique whereby the Allies would fire artillery shells just over the heads of their own advancing troops to land in the enemy's trenches just before the Canadians arrived.

The combination of weeks of pummelling by the pre-attack artillery barrage that caused sleep deprivation

Shelling the German positions on the ridge went on day and night.

and shell shock, along with the pinpoint explosions that prevented the preparation of a proper defence, left many of the German soldiers dazed, terrified, and ready to surrender.

However, very few battles go exactly according to plan. While the weeks of intensive training and the support of heavy shelling would provide the attacking Canadian troops with a tremendous advantage, the battle-hardened

Lt.-Col. Andrew McNaughton thought that barbed wire could be broken up by ground-level mortar bursts. He was right.

Germans were still a formidable enemy. As zero hour approached in the early morning of Easter Monday, April 9, 1917, a momentous battle was shaping up. It would forever change the widely held opinion that the Dominion of Canada was nothing more than a satellite of Great Britain and a source of expendable front-line troops whenever the British lion went off to war.

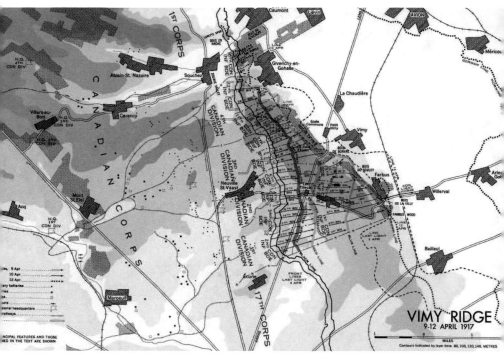

A map showing the Canadians' progress during the battle, compiled and drawn by Canada's Historical Section of the General Staff, Department of National Defence.

The success or failure of this massive undertaking, now that all the preparations had been made, hinged on each division accomplishing the formidable tasks assigned to it. The battle plan was a jigsaw of interlocking pieces, each dependent on the others.

Chapter 5
THE 1ST DIVISION

Private Bill Milne hoisted a bag of Mills bombs onto one shoulder and peered out into the darkness of no man's land. The driving sleet was threatening to turn into wet snow and transform the already treacherous mud into a boot-sucking gumbo that would make the troops' measured pace up the ridge all the more hazardous. Even worse, the corpses of thousands of French and British soldiers, who had failed in earlier attempts to take the ridge, were strewn in grotesque fashion all over the shell-pocked terrain.

But this was no time to dwell on these horrible mental images. Milne and the rest of the Corps committed to the Vimy assault had been practising for this onslaught for months on terrain behind the lines that was an exact replica of Vimy Ridge. Each man knew precisely what was expected of him and what to do if he suddenly found himself in charge

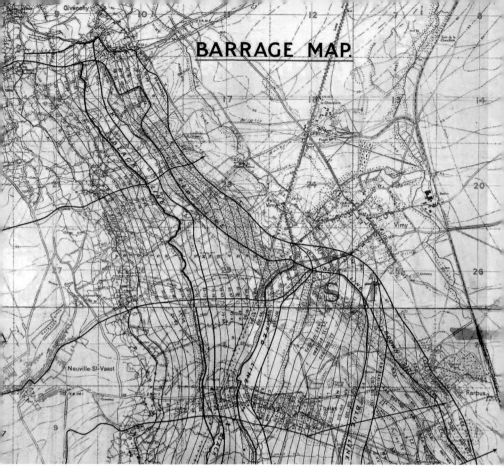

BARRAGE MAP.

This detailed map from 1917 shows the planning that went into the creeping barrage. Lines indicate just when and where shells should fall.

of his platoon in the event that everyone senior to him was killed or wounded.

The men were grateful to the Allied High Command for allowing each battalion and each brigade within the division to remain intact rather than being broken up arbitrarily in the traditional way. This meant that they knew who the guys next to them were. They could take pride in Canadians fighting beside Canadians and count on everybody around them to fight their hardest — if for no other reason than they didn't want to let their buddies down.

Stopwatch Attack

It had fallen to the 1st Division, including Milne's 16th Battalion, to attack the south end of the ridge from a position west of the Arras-Lens road and overtake the main enemy trenches in front of the shattered village of Thélus. A second wave would push through to Farbus Wood on the eastern slope of the ridge, where a sizable number of German heavy guns were hidden.

Rather than making a mad dash into deadly machine-gun fire, the troops had been drilled to operate by stopwatch. They advanced slowly toward the first line of German trenches in what was called the Vimy glide — a 100-metre advance every three minutes just behind a creeping barrage of Allied firepower, including heavy artillery and Vickers machine guns, that fired over the heads of the advancing troops. The barrage was designed to annihilate — or at the very least, discombobulate — those hapless enemy troops stationed in the forward trenches, tunnels, and dugouts.

Milne shifted his bag of grenades as the seconds ticked by toward the zero hour of 5:30 a.m. He and his fellow soldiers were loaded down with more equipment and weapons than seemed humanly possible to carry. In addition to the Mills bombs, each man carried a rifle and bayonet, 120 rounds of ammunition, an entrenching tool, 5 empty sandbags, 48 hours worth of hard rations, a waterproof sheet, a gas mask, goggles, a ground flare, and a full water bottle. In addition, the mud that had caked on their boots and greatcoats probably added another 30 kilograms to the weight they were carrying. Many of the Canadians had, in fact, elected to leave their greatcoats behind, despite the frigid

Every man had been taught what he had to do, on a mockup of the coming battlefield. Here, an officer gives the men final instructions before the battle begins.

weather. Others had cut off the bottom half of the cumbersome outer garment and had quickly been put on report for destroying government property.

The men had been assigned to platoons that contained a minimum of 28 troops and a maximum of 44. These units were organized into four sections of equal strength — riflemen, bomb throwers, rifle grenadiers, and Lewis machine-gunners. They would be controlled by a platoon command post consisting of an officer, a senior NCO, and two runners.

The Lewis gun was considered the most strategic weapon carried by the raiders. It was an air-cooled weapon that weighed just over 11 kilograms. Fed by a 47-round drum magazine, it could be fired from either a standing or prone

Canadian machine gunners with their Vickers guns dig themselves in, in a shell hole on Vimy Ridge. April 1917.

position. The routine that had been drilled into the men was that the Lewis guns and rifle grenades would pin down the enemy defenders while the bomb experts and riflemen attacked from the flanks.

As zero hour crept nearer, many of the troops suffered muscle cramps from being forced to half crouch in vermin-infested trenches, with foul-smelling water up to their knees, for most of the night before the battle. Their only consolation was the recent distribution of a generous tot of overproof rum, and, for those whose nervous stomachs could hold it down, a hot meal, such as it was. It would almost come as a relief when the shelling started, signalling the attack.

Right on the dot at 5:30 a.m., a blast, that someone later described as sounding like the screams of a thousand fiery banshees flying overhead, splintered the early morning calm. This Allied bombardment began obliterating the German front lines. As had been rehearsed so many times the participants had begun to grumble, the Canadians leapt from trenches and tunnels to begin their slow advance up the shallow incline of the western slope of the ridge. The 1st Division was on the extreme right, the 2nd and 3rd Divisions in the middle, and the 4th Division slow-marched along on the extreme left.

One of the first fatalities of the attack was Lieutenant Lisle Cradock Ramsay of the 1st Division's 15th Battalion. Having survived the brutal battles of Ypres and the Somme, this former Bank of Montreal employee was killed instantly as he led his platoon over the top with the first wave of his battalion. And in a macabre twist of fate, Horace Stokes of the 1st Battalion would lose his son, 16-year-old Private Stanley Tom Stokes, also a member of that battalion. The 40-year-old Horace would be killed just over five months later.

Another fatality that caused a stir back in Canada was the death of Captain Victor Gordon Tupper, the grandson of Sir Charles Tupper, a Father of Confederation, and Canada's seventh prime minister. The younger Tupper, who would receive the Military Cross for heroics on the battlefield, had insisted on joining the attack, even though he had been selected to stay in the rear echelon. He wrote home that if he were going to die, then dying on the battlefield would be worth it " ... a thousand times. I have 'been over' two or three times before, but never with a company of my own. Think of it — 150 officers and men will follow you to hell if need be!"

The 21-year-old captain was shot and killed instantly leading his company in a charge against a German-held position early in the assault.

Lt. Lisle Craddock Ramsay.
Killed near St. Eloi.

Despite their rigid training, some of the advancing troops in the first wave became overzealous and dashed forward, only to be blown to pieces by their own artillery. It also happened that the occasional shell fell short, with the same disastrous results. William Green of the 4th Battalion was witness to one such tragedy.

"An incident that stands out in my mind," he later wrote, "was when one of our own shells, which incidentally was a dud ... cut the head off a machine-gunner and took the leg of a lance corporal beside him."

However, the initial thunderous barrage was extremely effective, allowing the first-attack battalions of the 1st Division to reach their initial objective by 6:05 a.m. and dig in. As planned, the second wave leap-frogged ahead of the dug-in troops to attack the second objective, a long traverse trench the Germans called the Zwischen Stellung.

Heroic Acts

Here the German resistance proved much stronger and Private Milne decided he had to do something. Seeing his comrades in the 16th Battalion being mowed down by a well-entrenched machine-gun post, Milne jumped out of

Cavalry was used on occasion. The Canadian Light Horse goes into action at Vimy Ridge, on the south flank toward Willerval.

a nearby shell hole where he had taken cover. He crawled on hands and knees through the thick mud and got close enough to the enemy position to lob a grenade. His action silenced the deadly chattering.

Milne secured his hold on a Victoria Cross, the highest military honour awarded to troops in the British Commonwealth, by repeating this feat a short time later. Oddly enough, the wicked firing of a second German machine gun seemed to be coming from a haystack in the middle of no man's land. Since the Allied artillery had flattened entire villages and stands of forest as far as the eye could see, it was immediately apparent that the haystack was not what it appeared to be. In fact, it was cover for a concrete machine-gun emplacement and it was taking a severe toll on Milne's fellow soldiers. Once again, showing a total disregard for his own safety, the Scottish-born

A German machine gun emplacement in the village of Thélus.
That village was a 1st Division objective.

private crawled close to his objective and let fly with another grenade, destroying the gun emplacement and stunning the crew, which immediately surrendered to him.

Milne found himself in an awkward situation that many of his fellow soldiers would face during the attack. The German troops had been so devastated by the intense two-week bombardment and the morning barrage that, in many cases, they surrendered en masse, sometimes to just one lone Canadian. Milne and the others had orders to keep moving forward, so they simply told the surrendering troops to lay down their arms and head toward the Canadian rear area. Some of these dispirited Germans were pressed into service as stretcher-bearers for the mounting Canadian

German prisoners carry in a wounded 1st Div. Canadian on a board. Arleux, France, April 1917.

wounded or were handed picks and shovels and ordered to dig trenches for the advancing troops.

One of the many injustices of the battlefield is that, while some heroic deeds are rewarded, others go virtually unnoticed. One instance of this lack of recognition involved Private John Dunbar of the 10th Battalion who, despite several courageous feats just before and during the attack, earned not so much as a mention in dispatches for his efforts.

Dunbar had been part of several raiding parties sent out before daybreak on Easter Sunday. Their assignment was to check whether the barbed wire had been cleared away in front of the enemy trenches where they would be attacking the next morning. The Germans had detected the raiders early into their mission and were inflicting serious damage with heavy rifle fire and grenades.

Dunbar and fellow private Hugh Henry charged a position held by 9 enemy soldiers, killing 4 of them and taking 2 others prisoner. The entire operation was over in less than an hour, but resulted in heavy casualties to the Canadians, with 5 dead and 13 wounded. But the raiding parties had been able to confirm that the barbed wire in front of the enemy trenches in that section was still relatively intact and would be a lethal barrier to the attacking troops. The mission was thus deemed a success, because Allied artillery was then able to blast a hole through the deadly wire after the 10th Battalion withdrew temporarily from their forward trenches.

During the attack of April 9, Dunbar again performed heroically when the officer and all the NCOs in his platoon were put out of action by enemy fire. Taking over the unit, Dunbar led a wild charge in which he killed nine Germans by bayonet before being fatally wounded.

While Private Henry received the Distinguished Conduct Medal for his actions on Easter Sunday, Dunbar's self-sacrifice went unrecognized when it came time to distribute awards for meritorious behaviour at Vimy Ridge — a bureaucratic oversight that happens all too often in times of war.

Right On Time
Thanks to the bravery of Private Milne, Private Dunbar, Private Henry, and hundreds like them, the 1st Division was able to secure its second objective by 7:13 a.m., about one and a half kilometres east of the original Canadian forward line. Those troops who had made it to this second position had less than three hours to consolidate the area

before another creeping barrage began and the division's 1st Brigade, which had been held in reserve, would carry on to the next objective.

Just before 10 a.m., these reserve troops of the 1st Brigade, comprised of three Ontario battalions, marched through the line secured earlier by the entrenched troops. Their cheering and waving at their comrades as they moved forward soon turned to anguish as several tragic incidents occurred — caused mainly by the Allied artillery shells falling short of their targets and landing among the advancing Canadians. Nevertheless, they pressed on, and in less than an hour, they accomplished what so many experts had deemed impossible — they reached the crest of Vimy Ridge. Like in a scene from a Hollywood movie, the sleet and snow stopped at that moment, the clouds parted, and a weak early-spring sun shone down.

Some of the victorious soldiers would later write home about the jarring contrast that greeted them when they looked west down the battle-ravaged slope they had just fought their way up and then looked east at the untouched side of the ridge. Far below, they could see the grey uniforms of the retreating German troops. But what caused a collective intake of breath among the Canadians, who had for months seen nothing but mud, rotting corpses, and water-filled shell holes, was the idyllic scene below them of rolling green meadows, early spring crops, intact villages, and brightly coloured farmhouses with smoke curling lazily from their chimneys.

It was like gazing briefly at a picture postcard before a nightmarish reality returned. There were two more objectives to take. With the help of renewed shelling — this time on target

— they reached the third German position, called the Chain Trench, just after 11:15 a.m. They then had precisely 1 hour and 10 minutes to consolidate their position before moving ahead again. By 1:30 p.m., the 1st Division had reached its ultimate objective, Farbus Wood, part-way down the eastern slope of Vimy Ridge. The enemy was in full retreat.

It was now up to the 2nd Division to consolidate a hold on the German territory just north of this captured ground, so that the 3rd Division would be solidly protected on its right flank.

The Thélus Military Cemetery, in the quiet fields of France. Here, according to Veterans Affairs Canada, lie 116 Canadians.

Chapter 6
THE 2ND DIVISION

Sergeant Ellis Sifton ran a thumb over the sharpened edge of the bayonet affixed to his Lee-Enfield rifle. He knew from experience that the kind of battle he and his fellow Canadians were going into would include fierce close-quarters fighting. He would use his sack of Mills bombs to get in close to the enemy, but after that it would be bayonets and rifle butts.

The newly issued Lee-Enfield rifle was a welcome replacement for the old Ross rifle, a sporting piece that stubborn old Sam Hughes had insisted on making the official weapon of the Canadian infantry despite its tendency to jam after several rounds had been fired. A number of Canadians earlier in the war had been killed by enemy fire as they attempted to release the bolts on their Ross rifles with the heels of their boots or entrenching tools. Many of the troops had taken to picking up discarded Lee-Enfields from the battlefield after

Pack horses with ammunition for the 20th Field Battery, 2nd Div., Canadian Field Artillery. Neuville-Saint-Vaast, France, April 1917.

their unfortunate British possessors no longer had any need of them. The Lee-Enfield was a much superior weapon, but the by-the-book senior officers had followed Hughes' orders and demanded that the Ross be on each man's shoulder during inspection parade. That meant that many of the troops had been forced to carry two rifles into battle. Thankfully, saner heads eventually prevailed and the Ross ended up on the scrap heap, as did Hughes — but unfortunately not before a number of Canadian soldiers had been killed or seriously wounded due to the gun's deficiencies.

Sifton was a member of London, Ontario's 18th Battalion, part of the 2nd Canadian Infantry Division, whose task in the upcoming battle was similar to that of the 1st Division. The mission given to Sifton's unit, along with men from several other battalions, was to establish a foothold in the main German trench, Zwischen Stellung, after overrunning the German trenches near the ruined hamlet of Les Tilleuls. They would be followed by fresh troops, who were to join the attack on the German emplacements in front of the destroyed former village of Thélus. Once this position was secured, along with the taking of nearby Hill 135 by two attached British battalions, the Division's remaining attack force would head for Farbus to join their comrades from the 1st Division.

Sifton's 18th Battalion was part of the phalanx of Canadians that bolted forward from their trenches and tunnels as the 5:30 a.m. creeping barrage signalled the

29th Infantry Battalion, 2nd Div., advancing over "No Man's Land" through the German barbed wire and under heavy fire during the Battle of Vimy Ridge.

launch of the attack. It was tough sledding as they slowly advanced around and through gigantic shell holes, as well as mounds of barbed wire that had been blown to bits by the constant pounding of the Allied bombardment over the previous several weeks.

Like their buddies in the 1st Division to their right, Sifton and his fellow soldiers encountered a steady stream of dazed and demoralized German troops. These shell-shocked soldiers were only too ready to throw down their weapons and raise their hands in the air as they shouted "*kamerad*" and "mercy" at the onrushing Canadians. It was difficult to understand how these men had survived the artillery lambasting that had flattened everything in its path. The German trenches had been fortified with concrete, and a maze of underground tunnels had provided even greater protection, but it still boggled the minds of the advancing Canadians that anyone could have withstood such punishment.

The Canadians didn't have much time to think about these things, however, because some of the enemy's big guns were still intact, raining shells down on the advancing troops. In fact, the 18th Battalion received such punishment that out of the 1,000 men they threw into the attack, there were 600 casualties by the time the whole thing was over.

Perce Lemmon, a 19-year-old from Windsor, Ontario, was one of them: "It was a rugged fight, and this shell came over, and it hit over the side of where we were in this ditch," he recalled decades later in a documentary produced by the War Amputations of Canada. "It hit the hard road and the whole company went up in the air. I crawled out of 42 dead. That's where I lost my leg."

German 21 cm siege howitzer in a concrete emplacement, captured on Vimy Ridge. Graffiti on gun announce, "27th" and "WPG."

A Horrible Sight

Not only had many of the enemy survived the bombardment, the concrete pillboxes had also kept their deadly machine guns intact and Sergeant Sifton watched in horror as one enemy post in particular continued to mow down his men like flowers in a hailstorm. He decided he had to do something.

In the smoke and confusion of battle, Sifton spotted a machine-gun turret poking over the top of a German trench. Grabbing a couple of Mills bombs, he ran full tilt toward the trench and lobbed the first grenade at a section of barbed wire that had escaped the shelling and was forming a protective wall in front of the machine-gun post. Once the barbed wire had been put out of commission, Sifton continued his advance, ignoring the machine-gun bullets that ploughed into the mud all around him, until

73

he was within throwing distance of the German gun crew. The bomb did its job and as Sifton hurled himself into the trench, he saw the results of his handiwork. The entire gun crew had been killed.

However, a small unit of Germans began charging down the trench toward Sifton before the rest of his unit could join him. He managed to hold the enemy off with rifle fire, then bayonet, and, as he had suspected would be the case, the butt of his rifle, until what was left of his unit arrived and wiped out the remaining Germans.

The heroics of this one-man assault force led to the awarding of a Victoria Cross.

Another life-and-death drama was taking place around the same time in an exposed section of no man's land just to the left of Sifton's unit. Captain Robert Manion, the medical officer of the 21st Battalion, was attending to a wounded colonel in a shell hole they had tumbled into for the little shelter it provided. Shrapnel had opened up gaping wounds in the colonel's arm and leg and Manion was doing everything he could to stop the bleeding. The two officers were prisoners in a cage of hot steel formed by the rolling barrage of friendly fire to the east of them and an enemy bombardment pounding the old Canadian lines to the west.

Realizing that they would soon be caught between the pincers of exploding shells, Manion attempted to carry the wounded colonel, but they soon toppled into waist-deep mud. Summoning up his last reserve of energy, Manion began dragging his wounded fellow officer toward the Canadian lines at the rear. The colonel used his good arm and leg to help as much as he could and the two men eventually reached safety. Captain

Two temporary graves months after the battle, one containing L/Sgt. E.W. Sifton, VC. Two of his comrades from the 18th Battalion visit.

Manion later received the Military Cross for this selfless act.

Once the first objective had been secured and a mopping up action had rid the area of the last remaining German snipers and machine-gunners, reserve troops rushed forward and waited for the next creeping barrage to begin. This was their signal to push forward to the next objective, an area referred to by the Germans as the Turko Graben.

Schedule Met

Despite a number of casualties suffered by the second wave of Canadian troops, the next objective was secured, and by 9:35 a.m.— exactly on schedule — the 2nd Division's remaining reserve units were ready to march. A renewed creeping barrage of artillery shells provided deadly notice to the entrenched enemy that the Canadians were on their way.

When the 2nd Division's final goal was reached around noon hour, the various units had differing stories to tell. Some of them suffered heavy losses at the hands of stubborn pockets of Germans who were determined to fight to the death. Others were amazed at how quickly the enemy troops in their area of attack were ready to surrender. Still others were pleasantly surprised to find that the enemy had already fled, with ragged lines of German soldiers heading down the eastern slope into the Doui Valley.

As the victorious 2nd Division watched their comrades in the 1st Division to their right descending the eastern side of the ridge to attack the last pockets of Germans resistance in the Farbus Wood, a sense of pride began to wash over the troops. It was just beginning to dawn on them that the Canadians were within a few hours of accomplishing something that the French and British before them had not been able to do. They had overrun the solidly entrenched Germans on Vimy Ridge and, if their fellow soldiers in the 3rd and 4th Divisions were equally successful, this strategic rise of land would belong to the Allies after two bitter years of struggle.

Chapter 7
THE 3RD DIVISION

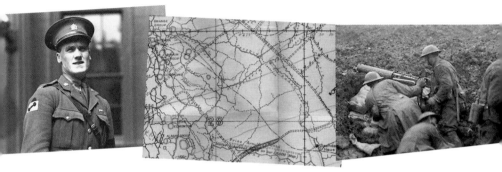

On paper, the 3rd Division seemed to have the easiest assignment of all four Canadian units involved in the Battle of Vimy Ridge. They had only two primary objectives to secure and the terrain they had to negotiate was just over 1,100 metres — not much more than a kilometre. Their final goal was La Folie Wood below the eastern slope of the ridge. The division's two forward brigades, the 7th and the 8th, overran the first three lines of German trenches on schedule in half an hour. Their second and final objective was achieved before 9 a.m. and it looked as if, after a bit of mopping up and digging in, the 3rd Division was home free.

However, intense sniper and machine-gun fire to their left began taking a tremendous toll on their ranks. The 4th Division had run into stronger enemy resistance than anticipated and had failed to take the heavily fortified

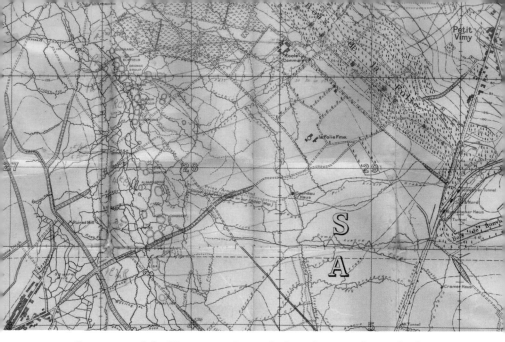

Base map of the Vimy area, drawn before the war, shows the farms, villages, fencerows and even trees in that quiet farming community.

Hill 145 on schedule. The Royal Canadian Regiment, the Princess Patricia's Canadian Light Infantry, and the Black Watch — the battalions on the left side of the 3rd Division's assault force — were suffering heavy losses as a result.

Obeying orders, the beleaguered troops continued to hold their position against a formidable enemy, taking whatever cover they could, and keeping watch for an expected German counterattack. One of those soldiers was Sergeant John MacGregor, a Scottish immigrant to British Columbia who fought with the 2nd Canadian Mounted Rifles.

Having been promoted directly from private to sergeant a few months after enlisting in 1915, MacGregor single-handedly captured a German machine-gun emplacement at Vimy, killing eight Germans and taking one prisoner. Leaving it to the men within his battalion to turn the captured gun against enemy troops still fighting in the area, MacGregor carried on up to the

*John MacGregor, VC. A natural leader and a ferocious warrior as a
sergeant at Vimy Ridge — and even more so later, as a captain.*

crest of the ridge and fired three white rockets to indicate that
this objective had been taken.

For his efforts, Sergeant MacGregor was promoted to
lieutenant and awarded the Distinguished Conduct Medal.
The DCM was awarded for exemplary conduct in the field
to warrant officers, non-commissioned officers, and lower
ranks serving in any of the Commonweath's military forces.
It was therefore the second highest award for gallantry
in action — after the Victoria Cross — for all ranks below
commissioned officers.

Despite the risk to life and limb of capturing the
machine-gun post, MacGregor later told his fellow soldiers
that his proudest moment was standing on top of Vimy Ridge
and signalling that this objective, once thought unattainable,
had been secured.

A Canadian highlander regiment, cheerful, going into the Battle of Vimy Ridge. April 1917.

A member of the 3rd Division not as fortunate as Sergeant MacGregor was Lieutenant Cyprian Thompson of the 7th Brigade's Royal Canadian Regiment. A former Bank of Montreal employee from Grand Mere, Quebec, Lieutenant Thompson had been killed on Easter Sunday in an operation carried out in preparation for the next day's attack.

Another tragic event was the death of two brothers who were also with the Royal Canadian Regiment. Once the battlefield had become silent after the chaos of the attack, the bodies of 28-year-old Private Wilfred Chenier and 27-year-old Private Olivier Chenier were discovered. They were later buried side by side in the Cabaret Rouge British Cemetery, one kilometre south of Souchez on the main Arras-Béthune road.

Until the 4th Division could regroup and capture the objectives set out for it, the 3rd Division would have to hunker down and do its best at avoiding the murderous fire lacerating it on the left. It was now a question of whether the men could hold on long enough for their beleaguered buddies to the north to gain the upper hand.

Trying to keep their heads down, Canadians with their Vickers machine gun dig themselves in, in a shell hole. That was all the third division could do: hunker down, and wait. Vimy Ridge. April 1917.

Chapter 8
THE 4TH DIVISION

Captain Thain MacDowell of the 38th Battalion was perhaps more aware than many of the other young Canadians waiting anxiously for the 5:30 a.m. shelling to begin just what was in store for them. The wound he'd suffered at the Somme the year before had healed sufficiently to allow him to return to the front lines in time for the Vimy offensive. As an officer, he had studied the intelligence reports and was aware that they would have to negotiate some tricky terrain. He knew they were in for a rough ride.

MacDowell had been given a medal in exchange for the wound he'd received at the Somme — the Distinguished Service Order. He'd earned it by knocking out three enemy machine guns and taking 53 German prisoners, despite his injury. Some of his fellow soldiers congratulated him on getting a "blighty" — a wound that would earn him a trip to a hospital in England and perhaps even a discharge and a return to Canada — but MacDowell was back at the front and ready to go into action again within a few months.

The Canadians would later learn that a combination of factors provided a recipe for disaster for the men of the 4th Division. For one, their section leaders had vastly underestimated enemy troop strength. As well, the battle planners had failed to realize that their troops would be sent out into the toughest terrain in the whole battle area.

The western slope at the north end of the ridge was much steeper than the gentler rise faced by the other three Canadian divisions. Not only did this make the attack that much more difficult, but the enemy's heavy guns were so deeply entrenched in the chalk tunnels that the shelling that had wiped out German artillery pieces on other sections of the ridge had been far less effective here. In addition, the Germans had been able to camouflage a series of concrete machine-gun posts on the far side of the ridge that would take a deadly toll on Canadian assault troops during the attack.

And Major Harry Shaw, acting commanding officer of the 87th Battalion (Grenadier Guards, Montreal), had been so confident his men would easily overrun the German positions that he'd requested some of the enemy trenches in the centre of the battle area be spared artillery bombardment. The theory was that these intact captured fortifications could then be used by the Canadians as a jumping-off point for their dash the rest of the way up the ridge. The request was granted.

Within minutes of the attack, the Guards would lose half of their unit from the firepower left intact in those unshelled trenches. Five officers were killed and another five

Edmund Ironside, Chief of Staff of the 4th Canadian Division, and his dog "Gibby," by a sand-bagged dugout.

wounded, leaving only one in any condition to issue orders. Shaw's tragic miscalculation threw the division's timetable off, causing a domino effect that adversely affected the other troops in the area.

The attacking soldiers of the 4th Division were split in two. Heavily armed German troops attacked with machine-gun and mortar fire from a middle salient, while other enemy fire from the well-fortified Hill 145 delivered the hapless Canadians a one-two punch. Being the highest point on the ridge, the hill provided the enemy with a deadly perch with a wide field of fire.

Bravery Under Fire

At this point, Captain MacDowell decided enough was enough. He had risked his life charging machine-gun posts before and he was prepared to do so again. Ordering two battalion runners to stick with him, he jumped from cover and silenced one of two machine-gun posts in his path by lobbing several Mills bombs into the trench. The lone surviving gunner from the emplacement next to the one that had been destroyed by MacDowell's grenades fled into a dugout.

A former University of Toronto varsity football player, Capt. T. W. MacDowell, VC.

When MacDowell reached the mouth of this man-made cave, he shouted down to the German to surrender. Receiving no response, the Canadian captain climbed down a ladder into the depths of the tunnel. Once his eyes had become accustomed to the dark, he started forward. As he turned a corner, he nearly bumped into two German officers and 77 members of the Prussian Guard. He was trapped. But, as one of the officers issued an order to his troops, MacDowell decided to bluff it out, calling back over his shoulder as if a unit of Canadian soldiers were standing by above.

The Germans took the bait and all 79 of them dropped their weapons and raised their hands over their heads. Continuing the ruse, MacDowell sent his prisoners in small

The Taking of Vimy Ridge, *by war artist Richard Jack, 1919. Bigger than 3.5 metres by 5.9 metres, it emphasizes the industrial side of war.*

groups up to the surface where his two battalion runners were waiting to dispatch them back to the Canadian lines. The Germans didn't know until it was too late that they vastly outnumbered their captors.

Even at that, one of the prisoners, when he reached the surface and found only two lightly armed Canadians greeting him, reached for a nearby abandoned rifle. It would be the last move he ever made.

For his cool-headed actions, Captain MacDowell received a Victoria Cross to go along with his DSO. In addition, he increased his prisoner tally to 132. He waited five days until reinforcements arrived before he went back behind the lines to have a hand wound properly treated.

MacDowell would go on to greater glory later in the war, as would another member of the 38th Battalion, Private Claude Nunney, a machine-gunner who repelled 20 attacking Germans at Vimy even though he himself was wounded. For

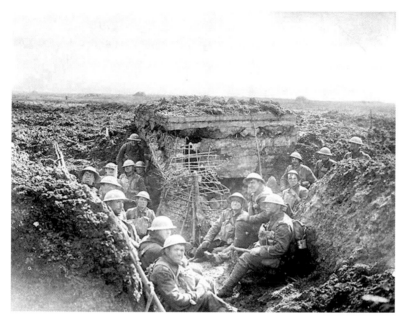

A machine gun emplacement on the crest of Vimy Ridge and the dirty, tired Canadians who drove the Germans from it.

his heroics at Vimy, Nunney was awarded the Distinguished Conduct Medal.

Despite the fact that the 4th Division had such a hard time at Vimy — or perhaps because of it — many tales of bravery about the men of that unit are recorded in the history books. Other members of the 4th Division who distinguished themselves on the first day of battle at Vimy Ridge were Sergeant Samuel Lewis Honey of the 78th Battalion, Private George McLean of the 54th Battalion, and Private James McMillan of the 87th Battalion.

Sergeant Honey, a schoolteacher from Conn, Ontario, had already won the Military Medal for gallantry during a raid on German trenches on February 22, 1917, for clearing

Private Donald Johnston McKinnon, No. 7 Platoon, 73rd Battalion, 4th Division, returning from the front line.

an enemy stronghold, then covering the withdrawal of his own and another squad that had come under heavy grenade fire. Honey won the Distinguished Conduct Medal for gallant leadership at Vimy. After his platoon commander had been wounded, he assumed command and led his men forward in the face of intense fire. Once dug in, they held their position until relief arrived three days later.

Private McLean had served with the Canadian Mounted Rifles during the Boer War at the turn of the century. After World War I broke out, McLean enlisted at Vernon, British Columbia, in October 1916 and was in France by December.

As part of the 54th Battalion's attack against the enemy

on April 9, 1917, McLean, armed with about a dozen Mills bombs, launched a solo attack on a group of enemy soldiers, taking 19 prisoners. Wounded in the arm by sniper fire, he still managed to stop five other German soldiers from reaching a machine gun, and so prevented untold Canadian casualties. For his bravery, he was awarded the Distinguished Conduct Medal.

Private McMillan, who had also served with the Canadian Mounted Rifles in the Boer War, joined the 87th Battalion of the Grenadier Guards at the age of 38 in 1916 and was almost immediately shipped out to France, where he took part in the Battle of the Somme. He participated in the taking of the Regina Trench and saw more than half of his battalion killed during that campaign.

That deadly history repeated itself at Vimy Ridge, where 55 percent of the reinforced battalion were either killed or injured. McMillan was credited with crossing no man's land twice to provide crucial information to the 11th Brigade. He was awarded the Military Medal for gallantry.

When planners miscalculate expected enemy resistance, a quick and drastic change of plans can sometimes save the day. With the Germans so well entrenched on Hill 145 and the Canadian units exhausted and their ranks decimated — about one in four of the attacking troops of the 4th Division had been killed — the totally inexperienced 85th Battalion was tapped to perform a miracle.

It was a desperation move on the part of the field commanders. The 85th, known as the Nova Scotia Highlanders, was a ragtag bunch of soldiers who had never before been in battle. An outbreak of mumps while they were still in England had reduced their number by about 200. The rest of the unit had recently arrived in France and had been seasick on the way over the Channel. To date, their weapons had been picks and shovels; they were trench diggers and ammunition haulers, not fighting soldiers. But they were the only fresh troops available.

Much to the surprise of everyone, including the Germans, the 85th galvanized into a fighting force and, under heavy enemy fire, captured the western summit of Hill 145 by the time the sun had set once again on this field of carnage.

Fresh Troops

In spite of this unexpected success, however, German machine-gun and mortar posts were still in operation on the hill's eastern slopes. The original plan had been for the 4th Division to gain control of the entire summit of Hill 145 by the end of the first day of the attack. April 10 had been set aside for final mopping-up action, including the taking of a small forested knoll British troops had nicknamed the Pimple, at the extreme north end of the ridge overlooking the village of Givenchy. But, with German troops still entrenched on the eastern slope of the hill, the attack on the Pimple — also known as Hill 120 — was postponed.

On April 10, fresh troops from the 4th Division's 10th Brigade were pressed into service to help finish the job their comrades had been unable to complete the day before. The revised plan was for two of the brigade's four battalions — the 44th from Winnipeg and Calgary's 50th — to operate from the trenches captured the day before. Their orders were to annihilate the German troops still dug in on the eastern summit

Elite Prussian Guardsmen, dug in, gas-masked and ready to fight, with their machine gun and long-handled hand grenades.

of Hill 145 and storm down the eastern slope of Vimy Ridge to the northern end of La Folie Wood at the bottom of the incline.

Fifty-six members of the 50th Battalion were Canadians of Japanese descent who had enlisted in the 175th Battalion back in Calgary when racially prejudiced units in British Columbia refused to accept them. The 175th was eventually sent to France as reinforcement for the 50th Battalion. Close to 200 Japanese volunteers fought overseas for Canada during the war and about three-quarters of them were either killed or wounded. More than 30 were killed in the Vimy area alone.

Sergeant Yazuso Shoji of the 52nd Battalion, which had been held in reserve and did not take part in the Vimy attack, was later asked why he and his comrades had been so determined to join in the hostilities. After all, it had been made perfectly clear that certain redneck senior officers didn't want them. "We don't forget what we owe to Canada and we were proud to fight when Britain declared war on the common enemy," was Shoji's reply.

Sergeant Masumi Mitsui, of Port Coquitlam, British Columbia, would win the Military Medal for Bravery at Vimy. A sandstone monument near Lumberman's Arch in Vancouver's Stanley Park would be dedicated to Mitsui and his fellow Japanese Canadian Corps volunteers on April 9, 1920, the third anniversary of the launch of the Vimy offensive. Mitsui's medal would be one of several wartime awards he would fling at a Canadian army officer confiscating his property during World War II following the Japanese attack on Pearl Harbour. He and his family would be forced to live in internment camps until that war ended in 1945. This unappreciated hero would later relent and take part in a ceremony in 1985 to relight the flame on the monument erected in 1920. The so-called eternal flame, housed inside a marble lantern, had been extinguished following the Pearl Harbour attack in 1941 and it would take more than 40 years for that sorry decision to be reversed. Mitsui died in 1987, five months short of his 100th birthday.

It took until mid-afternoon to get the two untried battalions into place and to formulate a new creeping barrage pattern to soften up the enemy as the Canadians advanced. That meant the attack force had the whole morning to do the last-minute things men do before going into battle. They read old letters from home, wrote new ones, checked and rechecked their weapons and equipment, or played cards to lend an air of nonchalance and stave off thoughts of the madness they were about to experience.

During this lull in the fighting, one member of the 50th Battalion, Private John Pattison, might well have been wondering what made him decide to sign up to fight a war that should have been left to those much younger than himself. At age 42, he was one of the oldest Canadians in the ranks at Vimy. He had a wife and four children at home in Alberta. He had given up a secure job with the Calgary Gas Company to sail to France and put up with despicable conditions in the trenches and the constant threat of injury or death.

Pattison had a double reason for enlisting. He was fighting not only for his friends and family back home in Canada, but also for those loved ones he had left behind when he had emigrated from England with his immediate family in 1906. And he and his fellow soldiers in the 50th Battalion had watched in horror the day before as German sniper and machine-gun fire cut down their comrades. The impending attack would help them avenge that slaughter.

When the heavy guns started laying down the rolling barrage early on the afternoon of April 10, the men of the 44th and 50th battalions began their slow advance toward the eastern slope of Hill 145. Once again, blistering machine-gun fire and mortar shells took their toll. The troops had to leave wounded comrades writhing in the mud as they leapt from shell hole to shell hole to try to gain some protection from the heavy enemy fire.

Pinned down in a shell crater, Private Pattison spotted an enemy machine-gun post directly ahead that was preventing his battalion from moving forward. With a sack of Mills bombs slung over his shoulder, Pattison braved bullets and mortar shells to make a run for the enemy stronghold. When he was within grenade-pitching distance, he quickly lobbed three of the "pineapples," as the bombs were nicknamed. The German guns fell silent.

Other members of the battalion moved in behind Pattison and together they charged forward, bayoneting any enemy soldier who put up resistance. By the end of the afternoon, in spite of a massive loss of men, Hill 145 was in Canadian hands.

The Pimple

Because of the change in plans, the Canadian Corps was given 24 hours to regroup and take a breather before launching a final attack on the Pimple, an action that would put the entire Vimy Ridge area in Canadian hands. Reserve battalions — British Columbia's 47th and the 46th from Saskatchewan — were brought forward to back up the battle-weary troops from the 50th Battalion who had hardly been given a chance to catch their breath from their ordeal two days earlier. With the prize almost within their grasp, the Canadians experienced a surge of optimism and pride at the realization that a horrible task had all but been completed. Even an overnight snowfall that covered men, equipment, horses, wagons, and weapons was taken in stride. The snow would undoubtedly turn to slush and make the upcoming assault that much more difficult, but there was still a sense that the worst was over — at least for the time being.

However, as ineffectual as its name might sound, the Pimple was a formidable target. The 120-metre-high escarpment was a maze of dugouts, tunnels, and trenches that earlier Allied attacks had failed to capture. And with the

The Pimple, Evening, *by war artist A.Y. Jackson, 1918. Canadians are advancing on the pimple. They attacked next day, in a snowstorm.*

Germans tenuously holding on to this last scrap of land on the ridge, the Canadians were well aware that the enemy's last-ditch efforts would be stubborn and murderous.

One well-respected member of the 50th Battalion, Lance Corporal Henry Norwest, a Metis of French-Cree descent from Fort Saskatchewan, Alberta, was taking advantage of the brief lull in hostilities by paying particular attention to his rifle and the telescope attached to it. "Ducky," as he was known to his mates, was the battalion's sniper and he had racked up more than 100 confirmed enemy kills so far.

At dawn on April 12, the troops of the three designated battalions emerged from their trenches and slowly followed the creeping barrage as it made its deadly march up toward the Pimple. Another snowstorm had hit, but the Canadians welcomed it since it was at their backs and therefore blowing into the faces of the enemy. It was almost as effective as a smokescreen in hiding the advancing troops, giving them an advantage that would help offset the fact that the Germans had also made use of the lull in fighting to bring in reinforcements. The new defenders were members of the elite Prussian 5th Grenadier Guards — all of them over six feet tall and formidable adversaries in hand-to-hand combat.

Nevertheless, within two hours, Hill 120 had fallen to the Canadians — but at a heavy cost. Nearly half of the troops who took part in the assault were either killed or wounded by the intense resistance put up by the enemy. The body count might well have gone higher except for the handiwork of Corporal Norwest, who felled a number of German troops during the assault on the Pimple. Norwest was awarded the Military Medal for his sharpshooting that day.

Brigadier General Edward Hilliam, a former Alberta rancher, had led the 10th Brigade in its assault against Hill 120. When his men had overpowered the Prussian Guards, Hilliam sent a report to Allied headquarters, signing it "Lord Pimple."

Chapter 9
A Bitter Victory

They had done it. Despite overwhelmingly negative predictions by everyone except the resolute Canadians, the taking of Vimy Ridge was judged a spectacular success by the Allied High Command — the single greatest accomplishment on the Western Front to date. But it was a hard-won victory, with 10,602 Canadian casualties, including 3,598 fatalities. German losses, under Colonel General Ludwig von Falkenhausen, were even greater, with 20,000 casualties and 4,000 captured.

Although the Allies expected an enemy counterattack, it didn't materialize and the Germans never again occupied this strategic site. It was later calculated that in this battle, the Canadians captured more ground, more guns, and more prisoners than any previous British operation on the Western Front.

The *New York Tribune* suggested in an editorial that Canada had fielded a better army than any that Napoleon Bonaparte had raised in the glory days of Imperial France. A French newspaper thanked Canada for a wonderful Easter gift. Legend has it that when a French officer heard of the victory, he replied, "*C'est impossible!*" Upon learning it was the Canadians who captured the ridge, he added, "Ah! *Les Canadiens! C'est possible!*"

As the Corps' commanding officer, Lord Byng, put it: "There they stood on Vimy Ridge, on the 9th day of April, 1917. Men from Quebec stood shoulder to shoulder with men from Ontario, men from the Maritimes with men from British Columbia, and there was forged a nation tempered by the fires of sacrifice and hammered on the anvil of high adventure."

The loss of Vimy Ridge caused the Germans to retreat to the lower plains, which were far more difficult to defend. Unfortunately, with simultaneous British and Australian attacks to the south of the ridge proving unsuccessful, very little of any strategic importance was gained in the area after the Canadian success. However, in a war in which thousands of soldiers on both sides were killed for the gain of a few metres of ground, the Canadian win gave a significant boost to Allied morale, while demoralizing German troops, who had thought the ridge impregnable. It also relieved the city of Arras from the constant German bombardment and the threat of imminent attack it had been enduring.

After Vimy

Following the Canadian victory at Vimy, Sir Julian Byng was promoted to a full general and put in charge of the entire

They did it! Happy Canadians returning to rest billets after capturing Vimy Ridge. May 1917.

3rd Army. His Vimy second-in-command, Arthur Currie, was knighted on the battlefield by King George V and promoted to lieutenant general. He took over Byng's duties with the Canadian Corps.

The war, however, was far from over. The Canadians stayed on in the Arras area and fought a bloody battle for Hill 70 during 10 days in late August. They took possession of a vital position on the northern approach to the city of Lens and managed to hold down the western section of the city.

Early in October, the Canadian Corps was ordered to prepare for an assault on the village of Passchendaele near the Belgian town of Ypres in West Flanders. The plan was to punch a hole through the German lines so that German submarine bases on the Belgian coast could be captured. Not only would this establish a strategic corridor, it would serve as a morale booster to the thousands of French troops on the verge of mutiny due to battlefield blunders by senior officers that had decimated their ranks.

The land on which the battle was to take place was largely reclaimed marshland, which had turned into a huge swamp after torrential rains in August combined with British shelling in preparation for the attack. The resultant soupy mud claimed the lives of untold numbers of soldiers who drowned after slipping beneath its surface.

To make things even more treacherous, the Germans were well entrenched and a vast number of machine-gun posts were still intact inside pillboxes that had not been destroyed by initial bombardment. It was literally a fight from shell crater to shell crater as the Canadians inched

German prisoners wearing gas masks bring in wounded. There are tanks in the background. Battle of Amiens, August 1918.

Stretcher cases waiting to be loaded onto the light railway. Vimy Ridge, April 1917.

their way forward under heavy enemy fire. On October 30, in tandem with two British divisions, the Canadians launched an attack on the village under cover of a driving rainstorm. Often waist-deep in mud, the attackers fought doggedly for five days until reinforcements arrived. Passchendaele fell to the Allies on November 6, but at a tremendous cost. By the time the Union Jack flew over the village, 80 percent of the attackers had paid for the victory with their lives, with the Canadians suffering 15,654 casualties. Nine Canadians won the Victoria Cross there.

One Canadian officer, Fred Holm of Toronto — who had worked out at his local YMCA to become fit enough to be accepted into the army — nearly ended up court-martialled because of an incident at Passchendaele.

Light railroad truck with a load of wounded on board. German
POWs carry another wounded on a stretcher. Vimy Ridge, April 1917.

Nine German prisoners his unit had captured were waiting
for transport back to an internment camp. Holm felt sorry for
them because they had been through a horrendous ordeal
and looked it.

Walking up to the first German in the straggly line they
had formed after throwing down their arms, Holm offered
him a cigarette. The prisoner, a Prussian officer decked out
in the Hollywood stereotype of crewcut and monocle, spat
in the Canadian's face. Holm, who had had his own share
of misery and near-death, lost his cool and pulled out his
revolver, aiming it at the offender.

"I don't know what I would have done," said Holm

Bringing in captured German officers. The Canadian success on Vimy Ridge was virtually complete. The enemy was defeated.

many years later, "if a young German at the rear of the line hadn't shouted out that he'd like one of my cigarettes. That defused the situation and I walked back to him, handed him a fag and lit it for him. In the glare of the match, I recognized him and told him so.

"The prisoner replied that he would have been surprised if I hadn't known who he was because he'd given me the best table every Friday night at the dining room at the King Edward Hotel back home. I immediately remembered him as the restaurant's maître d' and asked him what he was doing on the Western Front. He replied that he was German and had sailed home to sign up to fight for the Fatherland when he knew there was a war coming."

Whenever he related the story, Holm would wait for the inevitable remark that his was quite a small-world story, then he'd continue: "You haven't heard it all. I lost my leg at Passchendaele and spent more than a year recuperating in England. By the time I got back to Toronto, the war had been over for a couple of months. My buddies greeted my homecoming by reviving our traditional Friday night outing at the King Edward. And you aren't going to believe who the maître d' was when I walked into the joint … "

In a last desperate move, the German High Command launched an all-out offensive in the spring of 1918. Their troops got to within 70 kilometres of Paris and almost broke through the defences of the war-weary Allies. Somehow, the British, French, Canadian, Australian, and New Zealand soldiers found the strength to hang on and the German gamble didn't pay off. In fact, the tables turned on the Kaiser's troops when the Allies got their second wind under a new supreme commander, French Marshal Ferdinand Foch.

In a series of counterattacks, the Allies made advances throughout the Western Front. The period from August 8 to November 11, 1918 came to be known as Canada's Hundred Days. During that time, a contingent of about 105,000 Canadians made inroads of 130 kilometres. In so doing, they captured 31,500 prisoners, more than 600 artillery pieces, close to 3,000 machine guns and over 325 mortars. The price they paid was 45,830 battle casualties.

When the Allied advance began in 1918, the Canadian Corps was assigned to spearhead an attack on an enemy bulge in the lines near Amiens. This action led to the awarding

Later, after Vimy Ridge, a Canadian plays a mouth organ and his buddies listen. 87th Battalion, 4th Division, Amiens, August 1918.

to Canadian combatants of 10 Victoria Crosses. Advancing 19 kilometres in three days, the Canadians once again showed their mettle as shock troops in an attack situation. The German High Command was badly shaken by this feat. German General Erich Ludendorff called August 8 the "black day of the German Army."

Because of their heroic actions at Amiens, the Canadians were redirected to Arras and tasked with breaking through the enemy's main line phalanx, the Hindenburg Line. Between August 26 and September 2, the Canadian Corps slugged it out with tough German units and advanced to the Canal du Nord. With the aid of 15 British tanks, they managed to traverse this heavily fortified position. A breakthrough had finally been achieved. Victory was at hand.

Painted in 1918, Frederick Varley's grim For What? *shows a cart full of bodies collected from the Vimy battlefield.*

Cambrai was taken in early October. The Canadians then advanced steadily through Valenciennes and Mont Houy and arrived at Mons on November 11, 1918, the day the armistice came into effect. After more than four years of bitter fighting and tragic losses on both sides, the "Great War" was finally over.

The cost of total victory was high. Some 619,000 Canadians served in the army. Of all the Canadians overseas, more than 60,000 paid the supreme sacrifice. Canadian casualties totalled 239,605, one-third of those who had signed up to fight. Of 3,141 nursing sisters, some 2,500 served the many wounded on all fronts and 46 died.

Chapter 10
THE VIMY MEMORIAL

The Vimy Memorial towers over the Doui Plain from the top of what was known during World War I as Hill 145. Located about 10 kilometres northeast of the city of Arras, this is the highest point on Vimy Ridge. The inscription on the base of the monument reads, in French and English, "To the valour of their countrymen in the Great War and in memory of their sixty thousand dead this monument is raised by the people of Canada."

The immense and impressive twin-pillared monument is built on approximately one square kilometre of land donated in perpetuity to Canada by the people of France in 1922. Dominating the memorial is a 30-tonne shrouded figure carved out of one gigantic piece of limestone. She represents the spirit of Canada and honours not only the men who captured the ridge, including those who paid the supreme sacrifice, but also the 11,285 Canadian soldiers who died in France and whose remains were never found. Their names are inscribed on the monument.

Canadian sculptor and architect Walter Seymour Allward, who designed the monument, claimed the plans came to him one night in a dream. It took 11 years and $1.5 million to build the memorial. It was unveiled on July 26, 1936, by King Edward VIII of Great Britain, less than six months before his abdication of the throne so that he could marry "the woman he loved," Wallis Simpson.

Also present at the unveiling were French President Albert Lebrun and more than 50,000 — some estimates reach 100,000 — Canadian and French veterans and their families. On a pilgrimage organized by the Royal Canadian Legion, about 6,200 veterans, friends, family, and interested observers boarded five ocean liners and set sail for Europe, arriving in time for the ceremony. A further contingent of 1,500 Canadian vets living in England joined the pilgrimage in France.

Two future Canadian governors general and one future Canadian prime minister were on hand for the unveiling ceremony. Vincent Massey, the Canadian high commissioner for London at the time, brought along two of his staff. One of these aides was George Vanier, who, as a member of the 22nd Battalion, had been awarded a Military Cross for bravery after losing his right leg in a battle late in the war. Massey would make history as Canada's first native-born governor general, serving from 1952 until 1959. Vanier moved into Ottawa's vice-regal mansion, Rideau Hall, right after his old boss left the premises, and served as the Queen's representative in Canada until 1967. The other assistant accompanying Massey to the memorial unveiling was Lester Pearson, a former flying officer with the Royal Flying Corps, who had earlier seen action as a lieutenant with the Canadian Army Medical Corps. Pearson would win the Nobel Prize for Peace as Canada's external affairs minister in 1957 and would serve as the country's 14th prime minister for five years beginning in 1963.

The same foul weather the Vimy victors faced on that blustery April morning in 1917 gradually eroded the memorial to the point where the names of the honoured dead were, in some cases, obliterated. In addition, the fine statuary began to suffer wear and tear and the building blocks began to crumble as water seeped beneath their surface.

The main problem was that the architect had chosen a new technique for building the enormous monument by covering cast concrete with Seget stone — a white limestone found in modern-day Croatia. Unfortunately, no one foresaw that the two materials would react differently under inclement weather conditions. Differential movement over the years caused severe stress and shifting of the concrete and stone. This not only cracked the limestone but also allowed water to seep beneath the surface, further damaging the edifice.

Thus, the restoration of the Vimy monument was included in a major project announced by the Government of Canada in May 2001. A total of $20 million — two-thirds of the budget — was assigned to the Vimy restoration effort as part of the five-year Canadian Battlefield Memorials Restoration project. Veterans Affairs Canada, in collaboration with Public Works and Government Services Canada, assembled an international team of architects, engineers, artisans, and builders to restore the monument.

The stone from all the lower walls, stairs, and platforms was either removed or, if possible, repaired. The most deteriorated sections were replaced with the same Seget stone from Croatia. Artisans chiselled new sections where much of the old lettering had been obliterated by weather and by water seepage. New landscaping and lighting concepts were also implemented.

The craftsmen and builders kept up a furious pace to have the monument refurbished and ready to honour anew,

Left-front view of the soaring Vimy Memorial.

on Easter Monday, April 9, 2007, the sacrifices of the 3,598 Canadians killed at the Battle of Vimy Ridge. The memorial also acknowledges the more than 7,000 who were wounded, those who returned to Canada forever changed in body or spirit, and the 11,285 Canadians who lie in unmarked graves in France.

Legend has it that the 91.18-hectare battlefield park still claims the occasional victim. There are so many unexploded shells in the area that sections are roped off to prevent visitors from blowing themselves up by stepping on a live bomb, mortar shell, or landmine. In fact, the custodians of the park don't even allow lawn-mowing tractors onto parts of the site, preferring to allow grazing sheep to keep the grass trimmed. Every so often, the story goes, one of the beasts will step on a shell and suffer the same fate as so many soldiers did some 90 years ago. Even the shepherd is at risk. Several years ago, he stepped on a "mantrap," a sharpened spike that went through his foot, but he has since recovered.

And the site is also exposed to the occasional poacher. René Dubos of the nearby village of Vimy tells the story of a large truck being spotted driving up the ridge road under the cover of darkness a few years back. The next morning many of the "lawn-mowing" sheep had disappeared. A couple of days later, a festival was staged in the area with a massive barbecue featuring mutton roasted on spits over huge bonfires. René reports that

"Breaking of the Sword," a striking group of three young men, one crouching and breaking his sword, implies a defeat of militarism.

people came from miles around to take part in the festivities.

Since this massive monument to a great Canadian victory in World War I was officially dedicated in 1936, it seems to be a miracle that the structure wasn't blown to bits by the Germans under Adolf Hitler, who successfully invaded France only four and a half years later. Hitler ranted on a number of occasions, not entirely without justification, that Germany had been "stabbed in the back" when, at the end of World War I, the allied powers loaded the country down with unreasonable and inflation-spiralling reparation payments. So why did he allow this monument, signifying a massive German defeat, to stand?

Peter Craven, the senior technical adviser on the restoration project, offers the theory that the Commonwealth War Graves Commission, charged with maintaining the gravesites of Commonwealth soldiers around the globe, has always cared for nearby German war graves as a token of respect for the fallen of all nations. Hitler, apparently, was aware of this and left the monument intact. Even madmen, it seems, can have their lucid moments.

Epilogue
VIMY'S HEROES

It doesn't take long for a fatalistic cynicism to set in after exposure to the death and destruction of battle. The "luck of the draw" is an expression that war-weary troops have used in one form or another ever since the first armed conflict of any magnitude.

Upon seeing your best buddies — or total strangers, for that matter — cut down by a random shell or machine-gun burst, the usual reaction runs the gamut from shock and grief, to relief at having been spared, to the inevitable asking of the question, "Why them and not me?"

The luck of the draw is usually the answer. If asked to elaborate, the survivor will probably suggest that when your number is up, it's up, and there's nothing you can do about it. It's another way of knocking on wood to keep misfortune away — at least for the time being.

So, what was the luck of the draw for those Canadians who played a larger-than-life role in the capture of Vimy Ridge? Here's the rest of their story.

Lieutenant General Sir Julian Byng

English-born Julian Hedworth George Byng was 54 years of age when, as a lieutenant general, he was put in charge of the Canadian Corps in preparation for the Battle of Vimy Ridge. Following this decisive victory, he was promoted to full general and put in command of the entire 3rd Army. He would play an important role in engagements at Cambrai, Albert, Epehy, Havrincourt, and Valenciennes.

Photographic copy of a 1919 portrait of General Sir Arthur Currie by artist William Orpen, a portrait that Currie himself never liked.

At the end of the war, he was raised to the peerage as 1st Baron Byng of Vimy of Thorpe-le-Soken in Essex, England. From 1921 to 1926, he served as Governor General of Canada and was involved in the "King-Byng Affair," in which he refused to sign an Order-in-Council spearheaded by Prime Minister William Lyon Mackenzie King seeking the dissolution of Parliament and the calling of a new election. Instead, the Governor General invited Opposition Leader Arthur Meighen to form a government. When Meighen lost a vote of confidence in the House of Commons within a week, Parliament was finally dissolved and Mackenzie King was re-elected. Not surprisingly, Byng was soon on his way home to England, where he died in 1935.

Major General Arthur William Currie

Arthur Currie was born in Strathroy, Ontario, and moved to Victoria, British Columbia, as a young man. He joined a Canadian artillery regiment while still in his teens. His rapid rise through the ranks impressed his superiors and, with the rank of major general, he was appointed to command the 1st Canadian Division in 1915. After the Battle of Vimy Ridge, Currie was promoted to lieutenant general and succeeded Sir Julian Byng as general officer commanding the Canadian Corps. At 41, he was reputed to be the youngest officer to achieve this rank in the British armies. Currie was knighted by King George V in 1917.

After the war, Currie became president and vice chancellor of Montreal's McGill University. He died in Montreal on November 30, 1933, after a brief illness. It was estimated at the time that one-quarter of the population of the City of Montreal turned out for his funeral.

Lieutenant Colonel Andrew McNaughton

Andy McNaughton was well rewarded for his success in implementing the creeping barrage and in applying his scientific education to various aspects of enhancing Allied firepower and making the big guns of the enemy less effective. After Vimy, this native of Moosomin, Northwest Territories (now Saskatchewan), was promoted to brigadier general and put in charge of the Allied artillery for the duration of the war.

Remaining in the Canadian armed forces after the war, McNaughton had become chief of the general staff by 1929. In 1935, he was appointed chairman of the National Research Council but returned to the army to command the Canadian Forces at the outbreak of World War II. Late in 1939, he took the First Canadian Division overseas as a major general. He returned to Canada to become defence minister, but was defeated twice at the polls in back-to-back elections in 1945.

McNaughton was appointed to the joint Canada–U.S. defence board and then, in 1946, to the Canadian and United Nations' atomic energy commissions. He became permanent Canadian delegate to the UN in 1948 and, in 1950, was appointed to the International Joint Commission. He died in Montebello, Quebec, on July 11, 1966.

Baron Ludwig Freiherr von Falkenhausen

Colonel General von Falkenhausen was born in Guben, Prussia, in 1840 and saw action in the Austro-Prussian war of 1866 and the Franco-Prussian War of 1870–1871. When World War I broke out, von Falkenhausen was called out of retirement at the age of 74 to command Germany Army Detachment "A" from 1914 to 1916.

He received the coveted German medal "Pour le Merité" in 1915 for distinguished service in northeastern France. In 1917, he headed the German Sixth Army in the Battle of Vimy Ridge. Following this defeat, he was appointed Governor General of Belgium until the end of the war. He retired to Gorlitz, Germany, where he died on May 4, 1936.

Ironically, his nephew, Alexander von Falkenhausen, also received the Pour le Merité medal in World War I and was also named Governor General

Capt. R. J. Manion.
Won Military Cross.

of Belgium — in his case during the German occupation of that country in World War II. During that conflict, Alexander was involved in an unsuccessful plot to kill Adolf Hitler and spent the latter part of the war in concentration camps before being liberated by the Allies. He died in 1966.

Captain Robert James Manion

Robert Manion was born in Pembroke, Ontario, on November 19, 1881, and studied medicine at Queen's University in Kingston, Ontario, and in Edinburgh, Scotland, before settling in Fort William, Ontario (now Thunder Bay), where his parents had lived since 1888. In 1915, he joined the Canadian Army Medical Corps and won the Military Cross for saving the life of a fellow officer at the Battle of Vimy Ridge.

Upon his discharge from the Canadian army, Manion was elected to the House of Commons as the Member of Parliament for Fort William. Conservative prime minister Arthur Meighen appointed him minister of soldiers' civil re-establishment in 1921 and he later served as postmaster general.

Although he lost his seat in an election in 1935, Manion won the 1938 Conservative leadership race and re-entered the House of Commons in a by-election that year. His party lost the 1940 election and Manion was defeated in his own riding, leading to his resignation as leader. He died in Ottawa three years later on July 2, 1943.

Captain Thain Wendell MacDowell

Born in Lachute, Quebec, on September 16, 1890, MacDowell received his Bachelor of Arts degree from the University of Toronto in 1914. He enlisted in the 41st Regiment (Brockville Rifles) then transferred to the 38th Canadian Infantry Battalion.

During the Battle of the Somme in 1916, MacDowell was awarded the Distinguished Service Order for knocking out three enemy machine-gun nests and taking 53 German prisoners. Wounded in the attack, he recuperated in England and returned to France in 1917 in time for the Battle of Vimy Ridge.

During the action that won him the Victoria Cross, MacDowell sustained a hand wound but stayed in the fight for almost a week until relief

Capt. Thain Wendell MacDowell. VC.

troops arrived. Once again sent to England for treatment of his wound, he received his VC from King George V.

Unfortunately, the stress of battle caught up with MacDowell and he suffered a nervous breakdown in the fall of 1917. Invalided home, he spent three months in the Brockville General Hospital and was then pronounced fit to return to his duties. He served the rest of the war in England.

After a long career in Canada's peacetime army, including a stint as private secretary to the minister of national defence, MacDowell left the service as a lieutenant colonel and returned to civilian life as a director of several mining companies as well as president of the Chemical Research Foundation. He died in March 1960 in Nassau, the Bahamas, and is buried in Brockville, Ontario.

Lance Sergeant Ellis Wellwood Sifton

In October 1914, Ellis Sifton, a farmer born in Wallacetown, Ontario on October 12, 1891, enlisted in the St. Thomas Regiment but transferred to the 18th Battalion to go overseas the following year.

Sifton would never know that his action in silencing a machine-gun post single-handedly at Vimy Ridge would earn him the Victoria Cross. As he was holding the newly won position against a counterattack, one of the Germans he had mortally wounded with his bayonet was able to get off a rifle shot before he died, killing Sifton instantly.

The VC winner is buried in a mass grave in the Lichfield Crater Cemetery east of the community of Neuville-Saint-Vaast, near where he fell. The cemetery contains the bodies of 52 Canadians as well as about a dozen other soldiers whose nationality is unknown.

Sergeant John MacGregor

John MacGregor's story is a template for many other tales of heroism involving Vimy Ridge. Here was an NCO who was awarded a medal for bravery during this epic battle only to go on to even greater honours later in the war. In MacGregor's case, this meant earning several other medals, including the Victoria Cross.

The reason John MacGregor stands out from all the others is that, when hostilities ended, not only did he hold the distinction of having risen from private to captain in a little over two years, he had also been awarded more medals for valour than any other Canadian soldier in history. These included the VC, Military Cross and bar (the bar indicating he had won this award twice), Distinguished Conduct Medal, and the Efficiency Decoration.

What makes MacGregor's story all the more remarkable is that this leader of men had been virtually a recluse until he enlisted and became part of the 2nd Canadian Mounted Rifles. Born in Nairn, Scotland, on February 11, 1889, MacGregor had immigrated to Canada in 1909 where he worked as a cowboy and construction labourer before heading into northern British Columbia to take up trapping. It wasn't until March 1915 that he learned from a passing ranger that a war was raging in Europe.

MacGregor snowshoed out to Terrace, British Columbia, sleeping in snowdrifts for a week before reaching civilization. He then rode a freight train to Prince Rupert and went straight to the recruiting office without bothering to clean up. His offer to enlist was declined. He was deemed "unfit for duty in the Canadian Army." But the army hadn't counted on MacGregor's obstinacy. He took a boat to Vancouver, cleaned himself up, and was accepted at the next recruiting post.

After winning the DCM at Vimy, MacGregor was promoted to lieutenant. In January 1918, he won the Military Cross for capturing prisoners while leading a trench raid and soon after was promoted to the rank of captain. In September 1918, at the Battle of Cambrai, his heroics earned him the VC when he captured a machine-gun position, bayoneting four Germans and taking eight others prisoner. At the Honnelle River in November 1918, he received a bar to his Military Cross by personally doing the reconnaissance that resulted in the seizing of two bridges from the Germans.

Returning to Prince Rupert after the war, MacGregor operated his own fishing boat for a time before returning to the construction business. When World War II broke out, he enlisted as a private without telling anyone of the honours he'd received in the previous conflict. When his record was discovered, he was given the rank of major and took command of a training unit in Canada. He retired with the rank of lieutenant colonel and was awarded the Efficiency Decoration for serving in both wars and for 20 years of dedication to the military. MacGregor died in Powell River on June 9, 1952, and is buried at Cranberry Lake Cemetery.

Sergeant Samuel Lewis Honey
Born in Conn, Ontario, on February 9, 1894, Lewis Honey began teaching school at age 16 on the Six Nations Reserve near Brantford. He enlisted in the

Sgt. S.L. Honey, DCM at Vimy, VC at Bourlon.

Canadian Army as a private in January 1915 and had been promoted to sergeant by the time he was shipped to France with the 78th Battalion in October 1915.

After being awarded the Military Medal in January and the Distinguished Conduct Medal at Vimy Ridge, Honey was recommended for a commission and sent to England to attend officers' training school. He returned to France as a lieutenant and was awarded the Victoria Cross for heroic action at Bourlon Wood on September 27, 1918, after all the other officers of his company had become casualties.

After repulsing four counterattacks, Honey went out alone after dark, located a German post, and took a party to capture it. On September 29, he led his company against a strong enemy position and continued to display "the same high example of valour and self-sacrifice." He died of wounds he received during this attack.

Lance Corporal Henry Louis Norwest

Henry Norwest was one of the most famous Canadian snipers of World War I, achieving a confirmed kill record of 115 enemy soldiers. Born in Fort Saskatchewan, Alberta, Norwest was married with three children and worked as a ranch hand. He gained early fame as a trick roper on the rodeo circuit.

On January 2, 1915, using the name Henry Louie, Norwest enlisted at Wetaskiwin, Alberta, but was discharged for misconduct three months later after a wild drinking spree. Eight months later, he signed up again, this time in Calgary under a new name and was assigned to the 50th Battalion. Here his skills as a sniper were discovered. He was able to lie motionless for hours on end and camouflage himself so that German soldiers could walk within feet of him and never know he was there.

In August 1918, Norwest had a bar added to the Military Medal he had been awarded at Vimy Ridge, joining a unique group of about 830 members of the Canadian Expeditionary Forces in World War I to be given this double honour. But he never got to wear this new decoration. On August 18, less than three months before the war ended, Norwest and two of his fellow Canadians were searching out a nest of snipers when a German bullet smashed into him, killing him instantly. He is buried near the village of Warvillers, France.

Private George McLean

George McLean, a Native rancher from the Head of the Lake Band in the Okanagan district of British Columbia, had enjoyed a distinguished career with the Canadian Mounted Rifles during the Boer War in South Africa. When World War I broke out, every single male between 20 and 35 from the Head of the Lake Band volunteered for overseas service. McLean enlisted and was part of the 54th Battalion in France by December 1916.

Despite being wounded at Vimy Ridge, he managed to capture a number of prisoners and prevent a counterattacking group of German soldiers from recapturing a machine-gun post. He received the Distinguished Conduct Medal for gallantry in the field. His wound was serious enough to have him discharged and repatriated to Canada where he worked as a firefighter in the Vancouver area. He died in 1934.

Private Claude Joseph Patrick Nunney

Born in Dublin, Claude Nunney came to Canada as a "Home Boy"— an impoverished youngster sent overseas to find a better way of life. He lived in several foster homes before joining the Canadian army. He was sent overseas on May 23, 1916. After being awarded the Distinguished Conduct Medal at Vimy Ridge, Nunney's heroics earned him the Military Medal two months later. He was to win the Victoria Cross for heroic action near Vis-en-Artois during a heavy bombardment on September 1 and 2, 1918, preceding a German counterattack. Nunney left the safety of company headquarters to dash through the bursting shells to the company outpost lines, going from post to post to encourage the men by his own fearlessness.

The next day, Nunney was badly wounded but would not leave the field, running ahead of his advancing comrades and inflicting heavy casualties on enemy gunners, killing 25 of them in his rampage. Wounded a second time, he refused to quit but soon became so weak that he had to be taken to a Canadian clearing station by stretcher. He died from his wounds 16 days later and is buried at the communal cemetery at Aubigny-en-Artois, France.

Private James McMillan

James Irving McMillan was born in Lindsay, Ontario, on August 25, 1877. He fought in the Boer War in South Africa with the 2nd Canadian Mounted Rifles and returned to Canada in 1903. At the age of 38, he joined the 87th Battalion and fought at the Somme in 1916. He won the Military Medal for gallantry at Vimy Ridge and returned to Canada at the end of the war.

McMillan became a fisherman and died in White Rock, British Columbia, in 1965 at the age of 87. He is buried in the veteran's section of Sunnyside Lawn cemetery.

Private John George Pattison

The sad truth of Private John Pattison's participation in World War I was that he really shouldn't have been there in the first place. Born in New Cross, England, on September 8, 1875, Pattison, at age 42, was one of the oldest Allied participants in the Battle of Vimy Ridge. Furthermore, he was a married man with four children.

He moved to Canada with his young family in 1906, first settling in Rapid City, Manitoba, and then moving to Calgary where he worked for the local gas company. In May 1916, he enlisted in the 137th Infantry Battalion and was later transferred to the 50th Battalion in time for the Vimy offensive.

Pattison survived that battle but was killed, along with his entire machine-gun crew, a little less than two months later, on June 3, in an attack on a generating station at Lieven, near Lens, not far from Vimy Ridge. He is buried at Vimy's La Chaudière Cemetery.

Private William Johnstone Milne

A farmhand from Moose Jaw, Saskatchewan, William Milne was born in Cambusnethan, Lanarkshire, Scotland, on December 21, 1892, and settled in Canada in 1910. In September 1915, he enlisted in the army and was shipped to France the following year with the 16th Battalion (Canadian Scottish).

Milne was another hero who would never know that he had won the Victoria Cross. On April 9, 1917, after knocking out two machine-gun emplacements single-handedly and, in the first instance, turning the captured German gun against the enemy, Milne was seen later in the day falling wounded behind a small hill while continuing the attack. His body was never found and his VC was awarded posthumously. His is one of the more than 11,000 names inscribed on the Vimy Memorial of Canadians killed in France and buried in unmarked graves.

Native Volunteers

Lance Corporal Henry Norwest and Private George McLean were only two of more than 4,000 Native volunteers who served their country in World War I. Many recruits felt they were honouring a tradition set by their ancestors, who had taken up arms to assist the British against invaders in the War of 1812.

One of these was Cameron Brant, great-great-grandson of the heroic Six Nations chief, Joseph Brant. Lieutenant Brant commanded a platoon of the 4th Canadian Infantry Battalion. The 28-year-old lieutenant was killed in 1915 leading a counterattack against German trenches near Ypres.

Another member of the Six Nations, Lieutenant James Moses, served in both the infantry and the air services. As an air observer, he was shot down over France in 1918 and both he and his pilot were reported missing in action.

Corporal Francis Pegahmagabow, an Ojibwa from the Parry Island Band in Ontario, was the most highly decorated Native soldier of the war. "Peggy," as his comrades in the 1st Battalion nicknamed him, was awarded the Military Medal and two bars — one of only 39 members of the Canadian Expeditionary Force to receive this honour. A scout and a particularly sharp-eyed sniper — with more than 375 "kills" on his record — Pegahmagabow was also credited with single-handedly capturing about 300 German soldiers. While information is sketchy, it is believed the corporal earned his MM at the Second Battle of Ypres or the battle of Mount Sorrel in June 1916, the first bar at Passchendaele in November 1917, and the second bar at Amiens in August 1918. After the war, he followed in the footsteps of his father and grandfather and became chief of the Parry Island Band. He died on the reserve in 1952.

When the Prince of Wales visited the Brantford, Ontario, area in October 1919, he presented the Six Nations with a bronze plaque to commemorate the 88 of its members who were killed in, or as a result of, military action.

Esprit de Corps

Historians and military analysts overwhelmingly agree that a decisive factor in the victory at Vimy Ridge was the insistence by Sir Julian Byng and Major General Arthur Currie that the four divisions of the Canadian Corps be allowed to fight together.

This decision meant that friends and relatives fought side by side in the same unit, spurring them on to greater effort in order not to "let down the side." And, when the smoke of battle had cleared, the wellspring of pride at the job that had been accomplished carried over into civilian life after the war. Canadians saw themselves for the first time as an independent nation and this sentiment soon turned to reality with legislation loosening the ties to Great Britain and giving Canada a singular role to play on the world stage.

The following are the Canadian Battalions that fought together at Vimy Ridge.

1st Division
• Commanding Officer Arthur Currie

1st Brigade
• 1st Battalion (Western Ontario)
• 2nd Battalion (Eastern Ontario)
• 3rd Battalion (Royal Regiment of Canada, Toronto)
• 4th Battalion (Western Ontario)

2nd Brigade
• 5th Battalion (Saskatchewan)

- 7th Battalion (British Columbia)
- 8th Battalion ("The Little Black Devils of Winnipeg")
- 10th Battalion (Calgary)

3rd Brigade
- 13th Battalion (5th Royal Highlanders – Montreal)
- 14th Battalion (Royal Montreal Regiment)
- 15th Battalion (48th Highlanders)
- 16th Battalion (Canadian Scottish, British Columbia)

2nd Division
- Commanding Officer Harry E. Burstall

4th Brigade
- 18th Battalion (London, Ontario)
- 19th Battalion (Central Ontario)
- 20th Battalion (Central Ontario)
- 21st Battalion (Eastern Ontario)

5th Brigade
- 22nd Battalion (Canadien Français — the "Van Doos")
- 24th Battalion (Victoria Rifles, Montreal)
- 25th Battalion (Nova Scotia Rifles)
- 26th Battalion (New Brunswick)

6th Brigade
- 27th Battalion (City of Winnipeg)
- 28th Battalion (North West)
- 29th Battalion (Irish Fusiliers, Vancouver)
- 31st Battalion (Alberta)

3rd Division
- Commanding Officer Louis J. Lipsett

7th Brigade
- 42nd Battalion (Royal Highlanders, "The Black Watch," Montreal)
- 49th Battalion (Edmonton)
- Royal Canadian Regiment (Toronto)
- Princess Patricia's Canadian Light Infantry (Originally formed in Ottawa)

8th Brigade
- 1st Canadian Mounted Rifles (Manitoba and Saskatchewan)
- 2nd Canadian Mounted Rifles (British Columbia)
- 4th Canadian Mounted Rifles (Central Ontario)
- 5th Canadian Mounted Rifles (Quebec)

9th Brigade
- 43rd Battalion (Winnipeg)
- 52nd Battalion (Port Arthur)
- 58th Battalion (Niagara Area)
- 116th Battalion (Nova Scotia)

4th Division
- Commanding Officer David Watson

10th Brigade
- 44th Battalion (Winnipeg)
- 46th Battalion (South Saskatchewan)
- 47th Battalion (New Westminster, Vancouver, and Victoria)
- 50th Battalion (Calgary)

11th Brigade
- 54th Battalion (Kootenays, British Columbia)
- 75th Battalion (Toronto, Hamilton, and London)
- 87th Battalion (Grenadier Guard, Montreal)
- 102nd Battalion (North British Columbia)

12th Brigade
- 38th Battalion (Ottawa District)
- 72nd Battalion (Seaforth Highlanders, Vancouver)
- 73rd Battalion (Royal Highlanders, Montreal)
- 78th Battalion (Winnipeg Grenadiers)

On Land, at Sea, and in the Air

While Canada's principal contribution to World War I was the Canadian Corps, some 23,000 Canadians served in Britain's Royal Flying Corps and 1,600 of them died in combat. Ten of the 27 aces in the RFC were Canadian. At sea, 5,500 Canadians served in the Royal Canadian Navy and another 3,000 in Britain's Royal Navy.

The memory of the 48 infantry battalions that saw action at Vimy is still honoured widely in the Canadian army. The current units that evolved from the warriors who took part in Canada's finest battle of World War I emblazon their regimental colours with the battle honour, "Vimy 1917."

Today, the members of the Canadian Corps in World War I are among those whose memory is honoured at each gathering of Royal Canadian Legion branches across Canada, and at pilgrimages around the world, with the recitation of lines from Laurence Binyon's immortal poem "For the Fallen."

They shall grow not old,
as we that are left grow old;
Age shall not weary them,
nor the years condemn.
At the going down of the sun
and in the morning
We will remember them.

ACKNOWLEDGEMENTS

The author first visited Vimy Ridge in 1962 while stationed at the Royal Canadian Air Force Base in Metz, France, as part of the Department of National Defence Overseas Schools program. Gordon MacKinnon, a history teacher and World War I buff, acted as guide and was a wealth of information during the tour of the memorial. Gordon is also the source for a series of letters written by his uncle, who served in the Canadian Corps and was killed during the Battle of Vimy Ridge. The letters in this book's Appendix are from this series.

Another Vimy visit occurred when the author accompanied the Honourable Bennett Campbell, Minister of Veterans Affairs, to France in 1983 as his communications assistant. One of the 19 WWI veterans on that pilgrimage was the late Fred Holm, who related a fascinating story about one of life's "small-world" coincidences, retold within these pages.

The Veterans Affairs Canada website, as usual, was a valuable resource in researching material for this book. In addition, a number of VAC personnel were generous with their time and expertise. Among those are Hélène Robichaud, director of the Canadian Battlefield Memorials Restoration Project, Peter Craven, senior technical adviser on the project, Danielle Gauthier, project coordinator, Julie Daoust, and Lise Poirier.

The author found a great deal of worthwhile information in two books in particular, Pierre Berton's *Vimy* and Volume III of Norm Christie's *For King & Empire*.

Thanks go to Liliane Opsomer of the Belgian Tourist Office in New York City for helping arrange air travel and on-the-ground personnel during the overseas research. Air Transat was kind enough to upgrade economy seats to club class — a far more comfortable workstation. Rail Europe was extremely generous in supplying rail passes to allow research not only in the Vimy area, but also in Ypres, Belgium, and at several other World War I sites. René and Jeanine Dubos provided wonderful meals and accommodation in Vimy, and the rest of the Dubos family — Serge, Martine, Melody, and Marjolaine — made sure the Vimy visit went smoothly.

Special thanks are due Reverend Phil Miller of St. Andrew's United Church in Sault Ste. Marie, Ontario, friend and military expert, who bird-dogged answers to some of the more difficult pieces of the Vimy puzzle.

And a salute to old friend Jack Nadeau, whose father, like mine, experienced the horrors of war. Jack's dad, Robert Samuel Nadeau, served in both the British merchant navy and the Canadian army during World War I. He survived his ship's sinking, a bayonet wound, and a German gas attack. May they and their generation rest in peace.

BIBLIOGRAPHY

Berton, Pierre. *Vimy.* Toronto: McClelland & Stewart, 1986.

Christie, Norm. *For King & Empire: Volume III, The Canadians at Vimy April 1917.* Winnipeg: Bunker to Bunker Books, 1996.

Dancocks, Daniel G. *Gallant Canadians: The Story of the 10th Canadian Infantry Battalion, 1914–1918.* Calgary: The Calgary Highlanders Regimental Funds Foundation (Distributed by Penguin Books Canada Ltd.), 1990.

Rawling, Bill. *Surviving Trench Warfare: Technology and The Canadian Corps, 1914–1918.* Toronto: University of Toronto Press, 1992.

Worthington, Larry. *The Story of the Canadian Corps 1914–1918.* Toronto: McClelland & Stewart, 1965.

Answers.Com: *www.answers.com*

Canadian Encyclopedia: *www.thecanadianencyclopedia.com*

Canoe: *www.canoe.ca*

CBC Archives: *http://archives.cbc.ca*

Collections Canada: *www.collectionscanada.ca*

First World War Site: *www.firstworldwar.com*

History of Canada Online: *http://canadachannel.ca*

Royal Canadian Legion: *www.legionmagazine.com*

Talking Proud: *www.talkingproud.us*

Veterans Affairs Canada: *www.vac-acc.gc.ca*

War Amps: *www.waramps.ca*

Wikipedia: *http://en.wikipedia.org*

Photo Credits

INDEX

Photographic references appear in italics.